Life

IS WRITTEN IN PENCIL:

Finding Your Best Life in Plans B Through Z

MELISSA PANARA

Synergy Publishing Group

Belmont, North Carolina

Life is Written in Pencil:
Finding Your Best Life in Plans B through Z
By Melissa Panara

Published by Synergy Publishing Group, Belmont, NC

Cover by Arielle Torkelson
Back Cover Author Photo by Carolyn Capozzi

Softcover, May 10, 2023, ISBN 978-1-960892-02-7

For Michael and Natalie
You were always my Plan A. I love you both beyond measure.
As you live, learn, erase, and rewrite, I'll be right there with you.

For Trevor and Roger
The world is better—I am better—because you were here.

TABLE OF CONTENTS

DISCLAIMER

M y qualifications for writing this book are pretty simple: 46 years of good intentions and the reflections on my own life experiences. That's essentially it. You, in fact, have the same qualifications: a number of years on this planet and a collection of experiences from which you've learned. And as much as I hope something in this book resonates with you, I am sure you have something equally important to teach me. (When *your* book comes out, email me, and I promise to read it.)

In a more quantifiable sense, I have a Master's Degree in Special Education and twenty-four years of experience championing kids in a variety of educational settings. But the content in this book really comes from my evolving conclusions about human nature and what fosters a life well-lived. I don't have research data; I don't have longitudinal studies. What I do have is the contents of my heart and a life-long passion for supporting the well-being of young people.

Disclaimer, Part Two

Despite this book's title, I'm not suggesting that *everything* in life is written in pencil. That would be overboard. Many things are forever. For example, I will forever prioritize spending time with family and chosen family, caring for my body/mind/health, and helping people in need, especially in my own community. But in *most* everything else, I'm still finding my way. I'm still erasing and rewriting, learning and course-correcting.

In addition, you may discover a pattern in this book: I make a statement about some facet of living a happy life or something I have discovered along the way. Then, before the metaphorical ink has dried, I walk it back a little. Usually in the very next sentence. Something to the effect of "Now, this, of course, does not apply in every situation with every set of circumstances across every zip code and land elevation..." So please know that if such a hedge is *not* included, it is implied.

Of course, my observations aren't ironclad maxims. They all have exceptions, and with very little effort, I bet you can find some. But if you take these ideas in the spirit with which they are intended, you'll have my unending gratitude. And I'll even throw in my Aunt Mary Centola's sauce recipe as a thank you. I promise you've never eaten anything this good. (See Appendix.)

INTRODUCTION

> *"Open your arms to change, but don't let go of your values."* —Dalai Lama

It was the first week of June, and I had just bought a pile of graduation cards for the kids in my life who seemingly grew up overnight. In my mind's eye, they were still the superheroes and princesses who rang my doorbell every Halloween. Kids just slightly older than my own with whom we'd shared an elementary school bus stop or Cub Scout pack. Yet, there they were—multiple *Class of 2022* graduation party invitations tacked to our kitchen cork board. Just a little more validation of a phenomenon I'd experienced many times before: adults blink, kids grow, adults can't believe it.

As I began to fill out the cards, something stopped me. I noticed that hidden among the congratulatory words was the subtle message that the graduates should *now know*, with a fair degree of certainty, *what* they wanted to do and *where* that dream cultivation was to happen. Is this really what I wanted to say? The more I thought about it, the more I realized that I wanted to offer a very different message.

Don't get me wrong; graduations are wonderful, end/beginning milestones worthy of celebration. These rites of passage represent years of hard work coming to fruition and the well-earned ability to choose your next path. However, thanks to Dr. Seuss and the greeting card industry, phrases like The Sky's the Limit, Reach for Your Dreams, and Oh the Places You'll Go mark these occasions with a certain bottled-up anticipation. It seems we are congratulating the accomplished graduates and encouraging them to go after what will make them happy, but also hinting that it should be something BIG. "Your next life journey is waiting.... and we're all watching to see what that is." Our intentions are good, but I decided that we're missing a key ingredient here. We don't acknowledge the all-important do-over option. We forget to mention that the autobiographical pencil each graduate holds comes equipped with a beautiful, pink eraser. So I decided to return the cards and write my own.

Ultimately, my message was pretty simple. I wanted to encourage them to *try something interesting* and see where it took them. They only needed a heartfelt hunch, a pencil, and a good eraser. Should they decide to erase that initial choice and start something new, it would not be failing. It would be living. It would be learning and course-correcting. And it would probably make their lives more interesting. Because discovering who we are or where we want to go does not happen on a static, predetermined, one-size-fits-all timeline.

A (Pink) Pearl of Wisdom

Congratulations! You did it!
High school is through,
Once a Raider, Always a Raider...
now applies to you.
Will you travel, go to college
or take a gap year?
I hope your Plan A makes you
grin ear to ear.

But if it doesn't, your heart will know,
Reach for this eraser and give it a go.
Life is written in pencil, it really is true,
So erase that plan and write something new.

There are no straight paths.
No templates, no stencils,
But… good news!
YOU are the one who's holding the pencil.
So, write your life story,
including rewrites and edits,
Your happy life's out there,
but it may take a few tries to get it.

The detours and byways and Plans B through Z
Are what make this life interesting,
take it from me.
There are no mistakes, only alternate routes,
You'll arrive at your best life; I have no doubts.
So, get out there! Begin!
Put your mark on the world,
With your character, your diploma,
and your trusty Pink Pearl.

Ahead of each party, I printed out my poem and wrapped it in a small gift box alongside a brand new Pink Pearl eraser. Even though I was using it as a metaphor, it still seemed important to give them the tool I had now deemed crucial to a life well-lived.

We Always Have Options

I've held this belief for quite some time: *life is written in pencil.* Ask my husband, Mike, and our kids, Michael (sixteen years-old) and Natalie (thirteen years-old) and they will attest to the fact that I like to say this phrase. Probably more often than they'd like to *hear* it, in all honesty. It is my way of expressing a sentiment that, I believe, can be applied to many scenarios, big and small: we always have options. Think about it. We are certainly not powerless when it comes to making change in our lives. In fact, I think it might even be our superpower. Of course we want to honor our commitments and do our best to finish what we start. No question about it. But we are not zip-tied to what is making us feel unhappy or disrespected, either. We want to stay true to our ideals, but there are lots of ways to live them out. "You must continue doing the thing you're doing now" is written exactly nowhere.

Permanent Marker Stuff

Oprah's O magazine used to have a column called *What I Know For Sure*. Each month when my issue arrived, I'd flip to that page first because I'd always find something that struck a chord. "What do you know for sure?" was a question that late movie critic Gene Siskel asked in all of his celebrity interviews, and it resonated with Oprah when he asked it of her. You can probably answer that question a hundred different ways, but the way I interpret it, the things we know for sure are concepts that reflect our values. The ideas and beliefs that, in combination, make us who we are. The permanent marker stuff of life. Our deep-seated beliefs concerning right and wrong and human decency that become firmly established as part of us. They are not likely to change. In short, you're not going to erase the things that make you YOU. Everything else, I'd argue, is written in pencil.

At first blush, this belief might seem a little chaotic. Or possibly irresponsible. But even if you've never considered this idea before, I bet you have stories that point to its validity. Have you ever switched to playing a new sport? Changed your lunch table? Dropped a class? My guess is you are *already* using your beautiful pink eraser as a way of editing your story in real time—a tool you've used each time you've adjusted "what is" in an effort to boost your happiness or bring you peace.

Your Autobiographer Is YOU

I think most people would agree that life is a series of overlapping journeys. The formula goes something like this: by force or by choice, we try something new. Usually, it's something that interests or challenges us, and it can be as big as launching a new career or as small as trying out a new recipe for dinner. As we go, we endure some ups and downs until ultimately, we accomplish a goal, learn a lesson, or both. Then, before we have time to blink, the process starts again and a new journey begins. *And we go round and round and round in the circle game.* Thank you, Joni Mitchell.

If you are one of the lucky ones, many of these journeys will be joyful. You may get to travel the world, find meaningful work, or raise a child. Your efforts will be met with success and satisfaction. Inevitably, however, some adventures will not be as rewarding. There is no immunity to the occasional scraped knee, rejection letter, or broken heart. Even more bleak are those journeys that take you through times of illness, financial hardship, or grief. This is life: *the long and winding road.* Thank you, Paul McCartney.

The circle of trying new things and the adventures that result are what gives life momentum. It is how the stories of our lives get written. Or more accurately, how *we* write the story of our lives. And that is a very important distinction... and the point of this entire reflection.

As with most ideas, there is a caveat; I would be remiss if I didn't point it out. Erasers are standard-issue. We all get one. Because of this, changes other people make in their own lives will certainly affect us. Sometimes we have zero say in the matter at hand because someone else is using *their* eraser. Natalie's best friend moving to Colorado was a most unwelcome change in her life. It was probably the first time she'd experienced the downside of life being written in pencil and other people using their erasers. But that is the nature of it; we can count on the fact that our small journeys are continually starting, ending, or changing... but so are everyone else's. It's a shared human experience, and it is as guaranteed as taxes and laundry.

Overall, I believe that life being written in pencil is good news. It is empowering because what's written in pencil you can erase, and what has been erased you can re-imagine and re-write. Edits can be sweeping changes or tiny tweaks. And with very little exception, there is no limit to this cycle; you can continue erasing and revising until things feel right. Because when it comes to modifying the components of your life, the power is pink, beautiful, and quite literally, in your hands.

THE BLESSINGS OF
A BUMPY ROAD

> *"Do not judge me by my successes. Judge
> me by how many times I fell down and
> got back up again." —Nelson Mandela*

If life is a collection of journeys, then, simultaneously, it is a collection of bumps in the road. We can do our best to avoid them, but most of the time, we just don't see them coming. Most bumps jostle us a little, but we get our bearings and continue moving forward. Forgetting someone's name, bobbling our words when speaking in front of a group, getting a parking ticket. Other bumps are so startling or upsetting that we have to pull over and catch our breath. Losing a job, ending a relationship, enduring a betrayal. Sometimes we hit a *series* of bumps that, in a cumulative way, wear us down and challenge our well-being.

You might be thinking, "How does this connect to all that Pink Pearl talk?" Good question, and I am glad to see you're still with me on that. All the while, as life jostles and bobbles us, our beautiful pink erasers remain in our pockets. These unsung heroes are "on deck" for you sports fans, or "waiting in the wings" for my theater peeps. This is because erasing, by nature, is reactive. It's an after-the-fact choice.

Good or bad, we can't proactively erase what hasn't happened yet. And there is something vital that connects the bump and the eraser: the takeaway. Allow me to explain.

My elementary school principal, Irene Smithwick Nadler, said this at my sixth-grade graduation in June of 1988: *The difference between stumbling blocks and stepping stones is how you use them.* Maybe she was quoting or paraphrasing someone else, but in my heart, she gets the credit. In my head, I can still hear her voice saying it, and even as an eleven-year-old kid, I knew that it was a very important idea.

I think Mrs. Smithwick was saying that the very same things that can break us down can also build us up. They can give us strength, clarity, and motivation. This is the magic of duality: two sides of the same proverbial coin. Bump on one side, takeaway on the other. Not to say that *every* disappointment or challenge has an upside. Sometimes things just go wrong; game over, end scene. But I would assert that the majority of life's bumps come with a blessing. A takeaway. Negative events can *teach us* something about ourselves and *steel us* for bumps yet to come. We just have to make it a point to flip the coin and see what's on the other side. We need to look for the takeaway and decide how we feel about it. Based on that, maybe we erase and maybe we don't, but, nonetheless, we have data (feelings, reflections, epiphanies) from which to make the decision. Therein lies the blessing. My friend Brian embraced this idea by tacking (probably his only) college rejection letter to his wall, not as a reminder of falling short, but as motivation to succeed in spite of it. The stumbling block became the stepping stone.

When he was in fourth grade, Michael was put on the B team in soccer. He had already played a few years on the more-skilled A team, so this placement was crushing. Initially, Michael would not even entertain the idea of playing on a team with less experienced players; *I have played soccer for YEARS, and some of these kids just started!* Being demoted (as he saw it) was a significant hit to his ego, not to mention an uncomfortable separation from his friends. Textbook bump in the road: *This was not the plan!* Ultimately, Michael did decide to play the season with this new-to-him team; the bump made him re-evaluate how important soccer was in his life. Turns out, pretty important. He didn't erase; he adjusted. Looking back on it now, we remember that season as one of unprecedented growth. Did he work harder to prove his worth, or would it have happened anyway, regardless of what team he was on? We'll never know. But we do know that Michael became a much stronger player that year. He started friendships with kids he still plays soccer with today. Being a more seasoned player, he also had a chance to be a leader, something that really suited his personality and was a source of confidence and pride. Michael has gone on to assume leadership roles in other areas of his life, and my guess is that he will continue to seek them out in his future. The takeaway.

My most personal story of extracting a blessing from a bump is the story of how my career first began. It is a story that, for many years, I was reluctant to share with anyone outside my trusted inner circle. But now, in the spirit of celebrating the validity of Plans B through Z and the power of the beautiful pink eraser, I am sharing it with you.

Steven Bartlett, the thirty-year-old entrepreneur, millionaire, and podcaster, is credited with saying, "Contrary to popular opinion, quitting is for winners. Knowing when to quit, change direction, leave a toxic situation, demand more from life, give up on something that wasn't working and move on, is a very important skill that people who **win at life** all seem to have." Steve, my friend, I whole-heartedly agree.

Year One: I Get Knocked Down

It was September 1999, and I had completed five-plus years of higher education. I was the proud owner of two degrees: a Bachelor of Science in Education (BsEd), which included a dual certification in elementary and special education, and a Master of Science in Education (MsEd) in special education for grades K-12. I was hired for my first teaching job in a small rural school district about forty-five minutes drive from my post-grad school apartment in Rochester, New York. In theory, I was as ready as I'd ever be.

My new job was in an ICT (Integrated Co-Taught) fourth grade classroom. I was the special education teacher, and my general education counterpart, with whom I'd share a classroom, was a very sweet woman who had been teaching fourth grade (and only fourth grade) for the last twenty-five years. In that very same classroom, in fact. I had a lot of anticipatory anxiety, but the determination to learn from my co-teacher and do right by my students was greater. After surviving September, I chalked up my continued nervousness to "it's my first year" and pushed through the discomfort. Unfortunately, my sweet, experienced co-teacher became ill and went on medical leave in October. I am happy to say she did recover, but she did not return for the remainder of the school year. Her long-term sub was a brand new teacher who was even *younger* than me. On top of this, we had a student-teacher from a nearby college. It was every bit the circus you are imagining, but our students were fantastic kids who gave fourth grade everything they had. I loved those kids, and to this day, could probably name them all from memory.

It was during this year when I first heard the saying "education eats their young." Definitely too "animal kingdom" for my tastes, but I understood the sentiment. Louder and clearer as the year went on, in fact. Allow me to provide you with this background: Best practice for the ICT model is a class makeup of one-third students with classified special needs and two-thirds students performing on grade level (i.e. with no specific learning needs beyond what is provided in a general education classroom). Our class of twenty-four had twelve students with documented special needs *plus* eight or nine students who were performing below grade level in reading and math. It was far from a formula for success. By January, I was noticing that it was becoming harder and harder for me to walk out the door in the morning. My heart would race, and I would feel tightness in my chest. I started watching Seinfeld reruns (on VHS tapes—yes, I'm that old) while I got ready for school in an attempt to combat the feeling and start my day with laughter and levity. It was a small attempt to address a big, unfamiliar problem.

For some context, I had always been a successful, high-achieving student. I am intelligent and hardworking, and I'd always had wonderfully supportive teachers. That little bit of anxiety I'd felt my whole life was nothing more than fuel to push me forward in school. It was manageable and probably a little bit helpful. My efforts as a *teacher,* however, were not met with similar results. I was taking care of my students socially and emotionally, but they were not thriving academically. Getting through it, but not thriving. With the same twenty-four hours in a day that everyone else gets, I definitely couldn't address everything on my daily to-do list. Not even close. There was just so much planning and prepping to do, and I was stunned at how much time it took to *do it well*. Not unrelated, I quickly learned that if students don't have an intact emotional foundation, the house of academic success you are trying to build simply will not stand. In hindsight, my inability to facilitate academic success was directly related to the help I was asking for but not receiving from my supervisors. I felt like I was treading water, just trying to keep my head from going under. I was protecting my student's wellness to the detriment of my own. Ultimately, the bump-filled year yielded the takeaway, and I Pink Pearled my way out of the situation. I was able to secure a job in another district for the following year. I thought a fresh start and a more supportive administration was what I needed. This first year was going to be a fluke in what was sure to be a long and successful teaching career.

Year Two: But I Get Up Again

New job, new district! Closer to home! Here we go! This time I was hired to teach in a self-contained, 15:1:1+ classroom for grades three and four in a nearby suburban district. This meant that there would be fifteen students (all with classified special needs), one teacher (me), one-plus paraprofessionals (*aka* two). This was going to be it! Spoiler alert: It wasn't.

I came back that fall with lots of optimism and energy. I set up my classroom to be an inviting-but-not-overwhelming haven of learning and support. My fifteen students came to me with a wide range of learner profiles. Surprisingly wide. Some were academically on or close to grade level, but had significant emotional needs stemming from one trauma or another. Meaningful participation in learning was far from an everyday occurrence for these friends; school appropriate behavior, not academics, took the forefront. It became commonplace to evacuate my students to an unused classroom down the hall to keep them safe from being hit by thrown chairs and the like. At the other end of the dial, I had students who were as socially appropriate and emotionally regulated as could be; they just couldn't yet read or count with one-to-one correspondence. To add to the challenge, I was teaching children in two grades. I was responsible for covering all of the social studies and science units for *both* third and fourth grade. Double the content area curricula. Also, because they went to "specials" (art, music, physical education—classes I was not responsible for teaching) at different times in order to stay with their grade-mates, I never had an empty classroom during my planning time like other teachers did. And I had SO much planning to do; the lesson prep with the needed individual modifications nearly did me in.

Finally, having two paraprofessionals for our classroom proved to be more work and less help than I thought. Not only was I writing lesson plans for a huge range of academic levels in every subject, every day, I needed to plan for the paras as well. It was part of my job to make sure they knew *what* to do to support our students and also *how* to do it (read: not doing it for them). And when I needed to gently correct those, albeit innocent, missteps, it was not taken well. These particular paras had each been moved from building to building in the district in an attempt to find a teacher with whom they could mesh, and they didn't take kindly to a twenty-three-year-old telling them that they needed to "do it this way." Needless to say, there were not enough hours in the day to address and accomplish everything on my ungodly to-do list. I went to school in the dark, I came home in the dark. Over the course of this year, it became increasingly difficult to think about anything else but my job. I was still in the "I'm going to do it all because these kids need me" phase. I told myself that all new teachers go through this and it would get easier; I just had to continue to work hard and bide my time.

It had not yet occurred to me (and wouldn't for YEARS) that I was, essentially, set up to fail. Yes, my students needed me: a dedicated teacher. But, just as much, they needed an administration adept enough to support new teachers and the awareness to not overload one class with such need that it couldn't be managed. Requests for help and guidance were met with additional items to add to my to-do list. "Do more," I was told. Education eats their young, and once again, I was on the menu.

Years Three to Seven: You're Never Gonna Keep Me Down!

Don't worry; I am not going to chronicle each year of my teaching career in vivid and draining detail. Quite frankly, I think I blocked a lot of it out as a means of self-preservation. But you probably can see where this is going. First, though, I'll hit on some of the high points.

- Mike and I got engaged at the end of my second year of teaching in June of 2001. Planning our wedding did turn out to be a good distraction for me. I remember thinking *this* will restore my overall happiness and help me focus on something else besides school. And it did, for the most part. Our wedding was the summer between my third and fourth years of teaching, and it was thrilling to come back to school as Mrs. Panara.
- After one year in my new district, my class was changed over to a fourth and fifth grade multi-age class, so there was a three year span when I had a group of students as third, then fourth, then fifth graders. It broke my heart to send them to middle school; we had become like family. Those kids probably have kids of their own by now, but they'll always be ten years old to me.
- One of my students nominated me for Teacher of the Week as awarded by a local radio station. To do this, she had to write an essay about me, something I know was difficult for her to do. The fact that she was willing to write this essay, even though she

did not have to, meant everything. Right there, I had won. I did end up officially winning by the radio station's criteria, and I was interviewed on the radio (which was played live over the school's PA system). I believe I have the interview on a cassette tape somewhere. Again, I'm that old.

For these reasons and a hundred others, I wanted to keep teaching. I loved building kids up, showing them that "they CAN," and highlighting all the character and potential they had. But I was pretty worn down. And I bore the guilt of feeling like it was my fault. Nevertheless, these kids needed me, so Mrs. Panara pressed on through and lived out some scenarios that she'd just as soon forget:

- Being told by a student that he was going to kill me and then having him cut me with a pair of scissors (I would say stabbed, but I feel that that is too harsh and blame-laden for a good-hearted little boy who had endured enough trauma to fill ten lifetimes).
- On more than one occasion, chasing a child through the school parking lot and down the main road, terrified that he would be hit by a car.
- Enduring threats from a number of angry parents, the least scary of which was "getting my teaching license revoked."
- Having another school employee convincingly "frame" one of my students for doing inappropriate things that she, herself, was doing to me. The innocent child ended up being pulled from his familiar school environment by his angry parents (understandably so) while the employee, who did admit to the offense, faced no consequences.

Situations like these, on top of the mountain of daily demands involved in meeting everyone's academic and classroom management needs, had finally affected my physical health. My body said to me, "If you don't shut this down, I will." And that is exactly what it did. My ever-present anxiety went up a significant notch, and I began having full-blown panic attacks. One Columbus Day weekend, while visiting my sister in Boston, I was convinced I was having a heart attack. Fully convinced. I told her to take me to the hospital; it was that intense. I didn't end up going to the hospital, but I followed up with my general practitioner when I got home. I started taking an SSRI medication to help manage the panic, and after it built up in my system, the panic attacks stopped. I clearly remember my doctor saying, "This will be like putting on a raincoat, but it isn't going to stop the rain." Deep in my heart I knew that the "rain" was my job, but I wasn't yet ready to hang it up. If I was going down, I was going down swinging.

Happily married, Mike and I were ready to start our family. This joyous decision came with a scary caveat; to have a healthy pregnancy, I needed to wean off the anti-anxiety medication on which I had come to rely. I had to take off the raincoat and subject myself to the deluge of anxiety that I knew I would inevitably feel. The problem, I've come to understand, was not the anxiety itself. That was just the byproduct of being in a terrible work situation—for years. My body was trying to tell me that; it was practically screaming at me. Yet, there I was, back teaching amidst these challenging circumstances without any medication. In the timespan from 2003 to 2005, I became pregnant twice and miscarried both times. Although I was told that a different and easy-to-remedy problem had caused my pregnancy losses, I felt in my gut that the stress I was under was playing a role in preventing me from sustaining a healthy pregnancy. My body just couldn't do it all, and part-way through my seventh year of teaching, I needed to take a medical leave from my position. I was grieving, I was recovering, and I was exhausted. My body just said, "No more," and I finally listened.

As I said before, it took years (and subsequent job successes) to understand that the way my career played out thus far was not my fault. At the time I took the leave and ultimately resigned my position, I felt guilt, I felt shame, and I felt an overwhelming sense of failure. I chose to hide the details of my story because I didn't yet know who to trust with it, or even how I felt about it myself. Time gave me the wisdom to see that there really is no blame to cast, no personal failure to lament. I can say with 100% confidence that I gave teaching *everything* I had, even as student need went up, expectations without resources went up, and the administrative support to make it all happen went down. I was fighting a losing battle, and I was done giving my life to the fight. In order to choose the bigger life, I had to walk away. I took my Pink Pearl out of my pocket and erased Plan A. And it was one of the best decisions of my life.

As a result, I did get better. In fact, I was back teaching that very next September, but this time in a much more manageable setting. I spent the next two years teaching in preschool for gifted children. Quite a shift, but I truly loved teaching that age group. From there, I was hired to work on the education team at the National Museum of Play, teaching and adapting lessons for school groups who visited the museum. During the years I held these jobs, I had two beautiful, healthy children. And even though it was roughly five years without medication (including two pregnancies and two years of nursing), I had found a way to have it all: an enjoyable life, a beautiful family, and a comfortable and gratifying career. Hello Plan B.

And you know what? It didn't have to be this hard. It just didn't. Here's my takeaway from the most challenging series of bumps in my road to date: What if I had given myself permission to *let go of* Plan A sooner? Maybe it wasn't a failure, but it certainly wasn't a fit. When I think about all the time I lost to relentless anxiety and debilitating panic, I feel something akin to grief. With a palpable intensity, I want those years back so I can *enjoy* them. Only now can I see that, even though I was trapped in a prison of my own construction, I always had the (beautiful pink) key. Like Dorothy and her ruby slippers, I had the ability all along. Instead, more than half of my twenties were spent in survival mode. I was working so hard to keep my discomfort at bay and press on because I thought I had to. I didn't have to. My time was precious. In doing the cost-benefit analysis, I thought about what I got from classroom teaching, but also what I had to give up to get it. For this series of boulder-sized bumps in my road, I had a salary and benefits, I had earned tenure, and I had met some amazing people (students and colleagues alike). But what did it cost? Seven years of a comfortable existence, which is way too high a price.

Given the same set of circumstances, you may have chosen a different path. My choices are the result of my experiences and the learning that followed. With my character, my diploma, and my heartfelt hunch, I went out into the world in 1999 and tried something I thought was going to be a fit. I gave it a fair shot. I had both successes and set-backs along the way, but, ultimately, I chose to change course. Among the lessons I'd learned, I came to a deeper understanding of grit, including its scope and its limits. Grit is what compels us to stick with difficult, worthwhile endeavors. It's where that one last push-up comes from. But we can take it too far. I took it too far. Even after I had exhausted my grit, it still felt wasteful or careless to walk away. So, instead, I came up with all sorts of reasons why I needed to continue. But none of those reasons were enough to carry me through.

Today I have a job in education that I didn't even know existed when I was in college. Through child-directed, one-to-one play sessions in school, I support the well-being of K-2 students. As a result, children feel better about coming to school; they build confidence and gain language to identify their feelings and get their needs met. I now get to *help build* that very foundation on top of which other teachers can build academic success. I can do my favorite part without having to be everything to everyone. It took two jobs in public education, one job in a private school, one job at a museum, and one job working for a local nonprofit to inch ever closer to what I wanted all along. I just didn't know it existed.

For me, my specific jobs in classroom teaching were a burden. It took a good deal of erasing and rewriting to find my current job, one that I consider to be a privilege. Quite a shift, but proof positive that everything will be alright in the end... because if it's not alright, it's not the end. My bumpy road took a very complicated and painful detour, but as it turns out, I ended up just one neighborhood over. Or in my case, just down the hall.

Since there is a greater-than-average chance we have not met, I don't know where you are in drafting the plans for your life. Maybe you are still in high school, just starting to think about what could come next. Maybe you are in your first post-college position in your field (how exciting!), or a good-enough-for-now hold over job while you wait for the right opportunity. If I may, I would like to offer up the following thoughts for your consideration: Think about what energizes you, what you lose track of time while doing. This is how you want to spend your time. Now think about what drains you. What exhausts you. Be on the lookout for this, and use mine as a cautionary tale. I speak from experience when I say that continuing to pour your heart and soul into a situation that drains you, even if it is honorable work, is not worth years and years of effort. "Draining" is not sustainable; it is at odds with a happy life. Look for ways to adjust—it may not be as dramatic of a course correction as mine was, but you owe it to yourself to do some erasing and rewriting. Your time is precious, too.

FOR YOUR CONSIDERATION

> *"I wish I could give you the answers, I wish that I could make you believe, I wish I could put you on your path and set you free. [But] that's what your heart is for. Listen to your heart."* —Edie Brickell

The above quote is a lyric from an Edie Brickell song that Tig Notaro uses as the "end credits theme" on her totally hilarious podcast, *Don't Ask Tig*. I highly recommend it, as I do all things Tig Notaro. Tig also has a podcast with Cheryl Hines called *True Story*[1], which I never miss. It comes out on Mondays, and I'm now addicted to starting my week laughing with these two.[2] But I digress.

The purpose of this tiny chapter is simple: I want to be clear in my acknowledgment that you have your own mind, your own priorities, and your own road to travel. And, the truth of it is, I can't learn something for you. You have to have your own experiences. Bobble over your own bumps. But if, while traveling, you come across something that can *facilitate* your learning, well, I think that is fair game. So, I invite you to think of this book as a resource, a jumping off point, or maybe even a

---

1   Hey, Snerkbols, hey! Listen to find out what the heck that means; you'll be happy you did!
2   No VHS tapes required.

counterpoint to your current thinking. In that way, my learning can help your learning. My takeaways, divided into five categories, can help guide your decisions. If you so choose.

As you read, you'll see that many times along my road, I've benefited from something that someone else has put out into the world. I am not privy to all the bumps that led these people to their takeaways or perspectives. They just modeled something that I found to be desirable or wise, and I was in the right place at the right time to witness it. And, believe it or not, you have been that person for others... even if they never tell you. They probably won't, but that doesn't dim the spotlight on what you've offered. What we put out into the world matters; it contributes to the unspoken give-and-take of the human experience.

Takeaway One

APOLOGIES: BIG, SMALL OR NOT AT ALL

> *"Your mistakes don't define your character. It's what you choose to do after you have made the mistakes that makes all the difference."* —Dave Willis

I f you are reading this book in order (and maybe you're not, you can have your own system; no judgment here) you know by now that I have been using the metaphor *bumps in the road* to talk about life's unforeseen negative events. But the more I thought about this comparison, the more I realized that there is a *subset* of bumps: our mistakes. The negative events of our own doing. The usually embarrassing, largely uncomfortable moments of poor judgment and/or self-centeredness. The blunders and mess-ups we WISH we could Pink Pearl into oblivion... but, sadly, cannot. Thankfully, though, we have a tool just as powerful as our beautiful eraser: the apology.

Little Kids and Big Offenses

When children are toddlers, we teach them to apologize for their inappropriate, albeit *age*-appropriate, actions. I'm guessing it is on

My Mikey, age three, August 2010

page one of the Parenting 101 handbook,[3] since we all know that we're *supposed* to do it and were definitely too tired to read as far as page two. Since all toddlers misbehave as they figure out the world, prompting them to apologize is bound to be a frequent event. Hitting, taking a toy away from another kid, pulling someone's hair—all just another day at the office for a typical two-year old. As a little guy, Michael would default to saying *I'm sorry* when I prompted him with the classic "What do you say?" even when the situation called for a *thank you* or an *excuse me*. Poor kid. Obviously, his apology was not completely sincere since I flat out told him to say it, but it was practice, nonetheless. You have to start somewhere.

Although par-for-the-toddler-sized course, this kind of apology is devoid of reflection. Michael was just too young to review his actions; he didn't feel remorse and then pause to reflect on what to do about it. (It is cracking me up picturing two-year old Mikey with his brow

---

3   If Mike and I were issued such a book, we definitely left it at the hospital.

furrowed, pointer finger tapping his angled-up chin, contemplating the fall-out from the shove he just landed on his cousin Taryn). His apologies at that age were just parroted sentiments: conjured by the adult, said by the kid. The offended party might feel a *little* better hearing this apology, but without reflection on the part of the offender, it is hollow and kind of meaningless. Because it is the reflection that motivates the other person to forgive.

One better than forced-parroting is teaching a young child the basic steps of apologizing. This usually happens when the offense is deemed "big," like when one child physically hurts another child. The two kids are brought together, and the one who did the hurting is asked to acknowledge what they did wrong, ask for forgiveness, and promise not to do it again. The kid who was hurt is prompted to forgive since the first child completed all of the basic apology steps. Bare bones, but moving in the right direction.

Bigger Kids and *Little* Offenses

As children continue to grow, their physical misdeeds taper off. Parents begin to see the last of the pinching and shoving, but the new, more varied mistakes of older childhood quickly take their place. But by this time, I'd argue, teaching our children how to apologize is already checked off the parental to-do list. *They know how to say they're sorry—they've been doing that on their own since Kindergarten. We've already taught them that. Besides, we're too busy limiting screen time to do anything else.* By not teaching older children how to apologize in a more sophisticated way, their requests for forgiveness can sound as hollow and devoid of reflection as when they were toddlers. Have you ever heard preteen siblings apologize to each other? That.

Here's another thing that can happen: an older kid's default setting becomes "defensive" because they don't know how to acknowledge and own a mistake. Admitting any transgression or lapse of judgment can feel synonymous with saying "I am a horrible person." I have vivid memories of giving my parents the attitude-laden *SORRRee*, not knowing how to graciously admit that I had messed up. My ego at ten years-old just could not bear the brunt of such an admission. Beyond this, perhaps an apology only feels necessary when it is a more large-scale offense, like the hitting/pinching scenarios of days gone by. But, of course, that isn't true. The vast majority of apology opportunities arise from the small, day-to-day errors of judgment. The little missteps of life.

> *"If you can admit it, they can forgive it. Both are freeing." —Melissa Panara*[4]

The Upside of Small Blunder Ownership

I'm not sure about you, but I make approximately seventy-one mistakes a day. Okay, I have no idea how many I make, but I know it is a lot. My heart is in the right place, as is yours, but it is situated inside a flawed, human person. Not to mention a tired, busy-but-not-good-at-multitasking person. But what I have found is this: these little missteps need only a short, remorseful acknowledgment and then life moves on. Easy peasy. Much easier and peasier than I ever thought growing up.

As the good-hearted, well-meaning person that I know you are, I am sure you have your own system for this. Here's the formula that works for me:

- *I See It:* Acknowledge the mess up. Let the other person know that I do, in fact, see the problem.
- *I Own It:* Make it clear that I understand that I'm at fault. There was something I didn't realize, forgot, didn't take into account, failed to see from their perspective, etc. The error was mine.
- *I'm Sorry:* The actual apology. I choose something to say from my personal list of small but mighty remorse-lets for the

---

4   I thought I'd throw one of my own quotes into the mix. Truthfully, I don't have quotes. I've never said this before now, but I kind of like it.

low-level but very common blunders of life. This is the clincher. The borderline-magical step that turns a potentially tense interaction into a manageable, relatable exchange. Feel free to use mine, but, since I'm a big fan of putting your own spin on things, I enthusiastically suggest that you grab a pencil and add your own.

- Yeah, that was not my finest moment.
- Clearly, I didn't think that through.
- Not the best choice, I now realize.
- In hindsight, that was not "the move."
- Seemed okay at the time, but now I'm not sure why.
- I really dropped the ball there.
- I wanted to circle back and say I'm sorry for....
- I honestly don't know what I was thinking, but I was way off.
- Yeah... that's on me. Sorry.

Even though they are short, statements like these are really powerful. I think you'll find that they diffuse tense situations by sidestepping conflict and avoiding defensive dialog. They are like water on a spark; no fire ensues. On top of that, these statements let the other person know that you are honest when it comes to your mistakes, which will build (or rebuild) trust. You will earn respect and be seen as a confident, mature person. You'll immediately get a raise and the corner office. Okay, not that, but it will open the door for others to own *their* mistakes and apologize to YOU. And with practice, these remorse-lets get easier and easier to say. I encourage you to try one at your next convenience, and because you are human, your next mess-up is right around the corner. It's okay; mine is, too.

Oh, and one more thing... Try not to water-down an apology with an excuse. This isn't easy, but I've learned that in the apology business; less is more. Let go of the urge to stick up for yourself. You might be tempted to include a "reason" to explain it away, but do this sparingly. The "I'm sorry I messed up but..." doesn't land the same way; it dilutes it. You can offer to *make it right* if the situation calls for that, but the reasonless, excuseless apology is by far the most powerful.

Wait, there's something else. Even after the apology is offered and accepted, you're still on the hook. You've got to prove you meant it. Future actions need to back up the apology. You've come this far; stick the landing.

Okay, this is really the last *one more thing*. I promise. (I think.) Laugh at yourself if the situation warrants it. Lots of mistakes can be pretty funny, and it just feels good to find the humor. So, to recap, *acknowledge and own the misstep, apologize, maybe add some humor, and move on*. And if the sky grows dark and lightning strikes, I promise it is just a coincidence.

No Apology Needed

In my life and on more than one occasion, I have been told to "stop apologizing." How did I respond to this? You guessed it. I apologized for apologizing. In an attempt to be a "nice person," I think we can develop a habit of apologizing for things *we didn't do wrong*. In fact, I'll go as far as to say we apologize for things that have nothing to do with us. Have you ever apologized for weather? I have. I mean, come on; was I really claiming responsibility for the *weather*? I can do a lot of things, but I am nowhere near that powerful. Al Roker doesn't apologize for a forecast-gone-wrong, and we shouldn't either. I think, to an extent, we are conditioned to apologize rather than express an alternate, more accurate feeling. Rather than remorse, are you feeling shock, disappointment, or frustration? Maybe anger, confusion, or exhaustion? Instead of forgiveness, are you asking for understanding?

So, while there are words we need to add to our vocabulary to remedy our missteps, there are different words we need to put into circulation when "I'm sorry" just isn't the right fit. We want to express some emotion, but we can do it without taking the blame. So, in order to address my Chronic Apologitis[5], I field-tested some updated phrasing, and you know what? I'm still a nice person.

---

5   Not officially recognized by the American Medical Association.

To put a narrative to this idea, here's a simple, real-life example. For years now, Natalie has claimed that the Halloween variety of Oreo cookies are *far* superior to the regular ones. Blind taste test results suggest that she really *can* taste the difference. (In case you are wondering, I cannot.) Knowing how much she loves these cookies and that they are only around for a limited time, I told her I'd pick some up on my way home from school. Whether it was distraction or autopilot, I walked in the door that day sans cookies. A relatable slip-up: I said I would do something but didn't. I should claim that mistake and apologize. And I did. Let's say, however, I *remembered* to stop, but I encountered an empty shelf when I tried to buy the Halloween Oreos. I did my job in this scenario, but it isn't my fault that the Oreo truck got stuck under a low bridge and never made it to Wegmans. Or that they are so delicious that they are flying off shelves all over town. I can acknowledge the feelings of my Oreo-less kid and ask for her understanding. I can offer a temporary alternative and make a plan to try again. "I was so surprised that there was not one package of Halloween Oreos at Wegmans. I know you're bummed, but I'll try Target tomorrow. We do have oyster crackers in the cabinet, though. Can I get you some?" Done.

When it comes to either our emotions or our values, I feel pretty confident in steering you away from offering an apology. As far as emotions go, you get to feel how you feel. Full stop. No one is entitled to put limits or qualifiers on that; emotions just are. If you are feeling something, there is a reason. If you are bored, you need more stimulation. If you are overwhelmed, you need less. Your feelings can be directives, but they are for *you*. You don't need someone's forgiveness for feeling a certain way. *I'm sorry I am too tired to go out tonight* can just be *I'm really tired from a long week. I hope you understand. Let's try for tomorrow night.* Because, truthfully, I am not sorry. I'm tired. I'm not even *sorry that I'm* tired. I'm. just. tired. In fact, I'm already in my pjs with the dog on my lap and the remote in my hand.

While feelings come and go, values are things you consider to be important over a longer period of time. Rarely, if ever, is an apology warranted for thinking something *has value.* "I'm really sorry that I like this" is a ridiculous sentence. For example, I value the practice of welcoming legal immigrants into the United States. If someone disagrees, I won't apologize for my point of view. I might opt to shed light on why I think offering a clear path to citizenship is beneficial for everyone. Or I might ask what information has led them to think that it *isn't* a good idea. If things are staying comfortable and respectful, I might opt to continue the conversation by asking what evidence/policy changes would they need in order to shift their thinking. And so on... but not to an apology. I don't want forgiveness, but I'd welcome respectful, intelligent discourse.

Somewhere along the way, I heard these wise words for the over-apologizer: Think about what you are sorry for, and see if the same sentiment can be expressed as gratitude. For example, "I'm so sorry I didn't get back to you right away" can be rephrased as "Thank you so much for your patience." It still gets the point across, but maybe you are more grateful than sorry. And gratitude is a feeling we want

My Nattles, age six, August 2015

to encourage—it is healthy to be grateful for other people's kindness, understanding, or generosity. Gratitude is associated with happiness whereas being perpetually sorry is, well, sorrowful. Let's not put ourselves through it, fellow recovering over-apologizers. We certainly know when to ask for forgiveness, but maybe not when *we're* the ones getting hit from behind with a shopping cart and then apologizing to the reckless cart-driver for merely existing on their path.

Letting Yourself Off the Hook

In my travels, I've come across people who handle guilt and remorse in some extreme ways. There are those folks who forgive themselves as soon as they say any version of the word "sorry," regardless of the response of the wronged. They never think about their misstep again. Then there are those who are so determined to spend all eternity "on the hook" that they go out and buy curtains and a matching bedspread for it. Of course, most people are somewhere in the middle, which really is the healthiest way to go.

Natalie is my big-feels kid. She loves deeply, is fiercely loyal, and super committed to what she loves. I think she gets these qualities from my sister, her Aunt Tara, who is the same exact way. So when Natalie messes up, she really feels it. I have said to her on many occasions, "All you did there (the misstep) was prove that you are human, and we already knew that."[6] I'm not sure if this has helped her feel better, but I try to think of it *myself* when I am in the throes of post-blunder embarrassment. We don't have to walk through life overburdened with regret and remorse. We can acknowledge it, feel it, and then set it down.

Life has shown me (and probably you, too) that, because our next mistake is right around the corner, we need to be able to brush off this one. I know this isn't easy if you are a live-on-the-hook type. You have high standards for yourself. That is admirable. And I get it; I am a recovering hook dweller myself. But ask yourself these questions: Was my poor decision mean-spirited or spiteful? Mostly likely, no. Have I

---

6   Hey, look at that. Maybe I *do* have quotes.

caused irreversible damage? Again, probably no. Will I remember it a year from now? Unlikely. Very few mistakes are on this level, but even if you answered yes to one or all of these questions, it is okay. We didn't think you were superhuman, and you are loved anyway. Finally, what would you say to your best friend or your child if he/she made the same mistake? I am sure you would be forgiving, understanding, and encouraging. Give yourself that same loving acceptance.

Forever and ever, life is going to present us with situations around which we feel remorse. Since we cannot erase our short-sighted offenses, I offer this vantage point for your consideration. Apologizing gives the other person a gift: the chance to forgive. Apologizing frees *you*, but forgiving frees *them*. You can't get more win-win than that.

Takeaway Two

BOTH ARE TRUE, AND THAT WORKS TOO

> *"You do you!"* —*Mackenzie Urbanski, et al*

When children are very young, they see everything in one of two ways: good or bad, right or wrong, just or unfair. Duality rules the day because, developmentally, this is how their little minds work. In tandem with this polarized thinking is the urgency of now. *Later*, *tomorrow*, and *next time* are too abstract and, frankly, of very little consolation. Have you ever witnessed a little kid being told, "Not today, honey. We'll get ice cream next time," and respond with "Sure, Mom, that sounds reasonable." Me neither.

During my preschool teacher days, I made it a point to think about this. To factor in this black and white thinking when setting up classroom routines, especially in the fairness arena. I can tell you with permanent-marker-level confidence that, at this age, *nothing* is more surveilled for equity than who gets to be line leader: the be-all-end-all holy grail of preschoolhood. Even with my planned, explained, and colorfully displayed rotation of line-leaders, students still told me, on the regular and with unwavering certainty, "Emily/Frankie/Lucy always

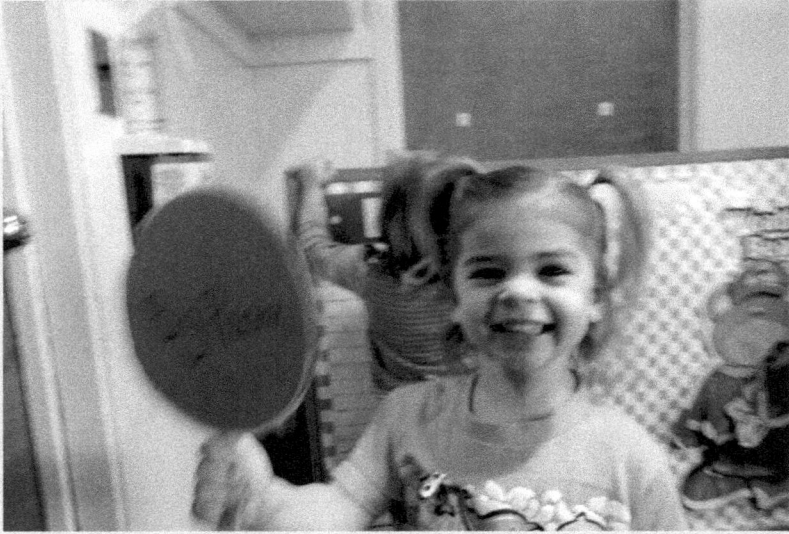

This is my Natalie at her own preschool (years after I taught this age). Just look at the pure joy on her face as she gets to be the line leader. Need I say more?

gets to be the leader. I never get a turn." Not now = never. When you are four years-old (or maybe an elected government official), *perception* of truth beats actual truth every time.[7]

As children enter grade school, however, they are increasingly capable of understanding that things aren't always so absolute (and that "later" does in fact exist). Shades of gray can be detected, so the word *sometimes* joins the well-worn *always* and *never*. Because of this, direct instruction in "flexible thinking" begins. Lessons with colorful characters and snappy catch phrases show kids the difference between having a "rock brain" and a "flexible brain." Maybe you remember learning this in Kindergarten or first grade. One indication that you are using your rock brain is that you've decided that only one thing is true. *This and only this.* Another is the assertion that there is just one right way to do something. *This way and only this way.* I know many adults who rock-brain their way through life, and I'm sure you do, too. Maybe

---

7   Expected behavior in the sand box; completely unacceptable in Congress.

you've even been one of them. You've probably figured out that, since I am including this chapter, I am no stranger to bouts of rock brain. And you would be correct. Good job... I knew you were sharp.

Just as weather and waves wear down actual rock, time and experience will erode the metaphorical rock of our rock brains. As we continue to mature, we can recognize that there are layers and nuance to almost everything. It doesn't mean we will *choose* to see things from a flexible vantage point, but the ability will be there in ever increasing amounts because more life = more perspective. People who give advice without being asked are good examples of people who choose *not* to see things from another perspective. They think they know enough to essentially decide for you because they have the (one) answer. They don't, though, take into account the fact that our experiences, preferences, and priorities might be different from their own. Rock-ola. I am sure you can think of someone who is *so* confident in their knowledge of the universe and humankind that they cannot *help themselves* from telling you "How things are." It is a service they are here to provide. Great, thanks. While thinking something very different in my head, I usually nod and say, "Hmmm, I hadn't considered that" or "I'll give that some thought" .... and then yell, "Okaaay, I'll be right there!" to the sound of exactly nobody calling my name.

Both Are True

People are complex creatures. Simplifying most everything down to "this" or "that" completely discounts that complexity. Opposites, though mutually exclusive by definition, can be true at the same time. For example, I think I speak for both Mike and myself when I say that vacationing with our teenagers is both wonderful AND draining. It is truly a blessing to spend a week together in a different part of our beautiful country, escaping the normal demands of day-to-day life. Simultaneously, the relentless negotiation involved in choosing a restaurant or picking a reasonable wake-up time can be an absolute joy-suck. I'm not sure if joy-suck is an actual term, but it popped into my head, and I think it paints the correct picture. On our last vacation, the distinction of "who is more miserable doing the other person's thing" was debated continually.

When thinking about the "both are true" concept, I can't help but recall my middle school years. If you are a middle school graduate (read: survivor), I apologize in advance for the flashbacks these next few sentences may evoke. With a foot in both worlds, I distinctly remember feeling like a little kid and a teenager at the same time. For Christmas in seventh grade, I was equally thrilled to get a pair of ZCavaricci jeans (super trendy at the time) AND a Pillow Person (a stuffed animal masquerading as a pillow or possibly the other way around). One minute I would be experimenting with makeup, and the next, building a blanket fort with my sister. There was confusion and self-doubt, a body very much in flux, and too much hairspray. Way too much hairspray. I didn't have to look any farther than the bathroom mirror to find proof that *this and only this* was actually *nothing/ nobody is just one thing.*

I can distinctly remember one of the first times I learned the *both are true* lesson about someone other than myself, and it was a doozy. Mrs. Tenenbaum was my seventh-grade art teacher, and she had a reputation of being strict and unapproachable. Art was not my forte, and she was very tough on me. My twelve-year-old rock brain had decided she was just mean—end of story. But, of course, I was wrong, because in simplifying my teacher down to one thing, I completely discounted the fact that her life had more than one dimension. It wasn't until May or June when I noticed it; the weather had turned warmer, and Mrs. Tenenbaum had pushed up her sleeves. Faded but unmistakable, a six-digit number was tattooed on her arm. She had been in a concentration camp as a child of World War II. All at once, she was a person with a past. And in this case, a horrifying and unthinkable past. My imagination immediately provided me with a black and white image of a young Mrs. Tenenbaum holding hands with her frightened parents as they were led out of their home by uniformed strangers. I tried not to think about the series of events that came next—what she witnessed, endured, and, ultimately, survived. Was she still a strict and sometimes intimidating art teacher? Yes. Was she someone who was steeled and shaped by one of the worst human atrocities of all time? Also yes. Nobody is just one thing. Mrs. Tenenbaum was *many* things as I came to discover when I found her obituary. If you'd like to read it, I've included it in the appendix.

Although the *both are true* concept certainly helps us understand each other as multifaceted human beings, it isn't limited to that. It can also relate to our ideas, opinions, and beliefs. Accepting more than one point of view as valid can be a tough pill to swallow, especially if you are super passionate about your take on something. Even if that something is a little ridiculous and of literally no consequence. Luckily for you, I have *just* the silly anecdote to illustrate this. Saw that one coming, huh?

Two of my high school friends had a debate that lasted literally decades: what defines a vehicle as a *car* versus a *truck*. You might be thinking, "How much passion could someone possibly have over the *minutiae* of car/truck distinction?" (You'd be surprised. Keep reading.) It all started because we were going on a ski trip during a college break, and we ramped onto a parkway with the posted sign: Passenger Cars Only. "What exactly qualifies as a 'car'?" someone wondered out loud. I don't think it was me, but I wouldn't swear to it. Opinions and supporting arguments formed fast. *An SUV is a car. No, no, an SUV is a truck. A pick-up truck is definitely a truck—it's in the name—but it does carry passengers. Doesn't everything carry passengers? Having a car chassis is enough to define it as a car. The trucks they *mean* are tractor-trailers. But the sign just says 'trucks'.* And so on for miles. Then across state lines. And definitely long after the rest of us had lost interest. But, at least on that day, we *had* to listen because we were trapped inside a moving car/truck/vehicle where the debate, in its infancy, was unfolding. As the world turned and the dispute raged on, there were degrees earned, weddings celebrated, homes purchased, and children born (just more people who had to tune out the debate). To my knowledge, neither one ever changed the other's mind with their limitless counterpoints and detailed "what if" scenarios. Even though I like to make jokes about its endlessness, the car/truck debate remains a funny and endearing memory highlighting two different perspectives that, in my informed-due-to-proximity opinion, are BOTH correct.

That Works Too

In addition to his day job, my brother-in-law, Jim, is an amateur movie maker. In our family, we often quote a line from one of his earlier movies: *It's my way or the highway for your way.* The line, though meant to be silly in its movie context, came to mind as a good way to describe our inclination toward thinking there is just one way to do something. We tend to think of *the correct way* as being singular. But the truth is there are lots of ways to do it right, almost regardless of what the "it" is. Your way *and* my way will each get us there... take the highway only if you want to.

This is a sign I made for my room at school. I quote it to my students all the time when they are trying to figure out how to do something. Sometimes I follow it up with "Keep playing and see if you make a discovery." The pride they feel in figuring it out themselves more than makes up for their short-term frustration when I won't comply with

their requests to "just tell me."

Back in 2007 when Mike and I first became parents, I was determined to do everything *the right way*. I think many new parents can relate, especially the overachieving, sometimes-rock-brained worriers among us. Even before the baby arrived, I researched the best car seat, the safest crib, the most popular high chair. Clearly, those models were the *right* ones. Once Michael was born, forget it. I drove my sleep-deprived-self crazy working under the assumption there was a *best* way to care for a baby. (*Oh sweet, well-meaning, A+ seeking Melissa.*) In hindsight, I can see that a few things in particular were feeding into my rigid thinking here. For starters, exhaustion and postpartum hormones had teamed up to make me, at least temporarily, the least reasonable person in America. In addition, there were all of those baby/parenting books; I owned way too many and had an unhealthy allegiance to all of them. Adding to that, I was fielding parenting advice from most everyone who crossed my path. And, although completely nonsensical, somehow the most recent advice I read or received became *the new correct*. Instead of regarding all this information as "many ways to do it right," I processed it as "Do only this. No wait... do only THIS. No no, hold on.. it's actually *THIS*..." Not surprisingly, what ended up happening was a sort of deer-in-headlights paralysis on my part. In trying to follow all these *musts* and *shoulds* to the letter, I didn't stop long enough to find my own way. To take a deep breath and listen to my gut. To simply observe my baby's patterns and make a loving, logical decision. Mike, at his wit's end (and, if you know Mike, this presents as mildly inconvenienced because the man rarely lets *anything* bother him) ended up hiding my parenting books somewhere in the garage. They are probably still out there behind some old cans of who-knows-what. He already knew what I needed to learn: that both "wrong" and "right" can be achieved in countless ways. He convinced me that all we needed to do was love our baby and figure it out together. We weren't going to ruin him. And, miracle of miracles, our kids turned out just fine.[8] Well, actually, way better than fine (in my admittedly-blinded-by-love opinion).

During my years as a suburban elementary school teacher, I had a tradition on the first day of school. Oddly enough, it

---

[8]   Shout out to Beth Anne, the nurse line nurse at our pediatrician's office. Your patience with me should have earned you the Nobel Prize for Reassuring Overwrought New Parents. I'm almost positive that that is a real award... and that you are a real person, not just a wise and soothing voice on the other end of the phone.

centered around shoes. Since lots of students wore new shoes on the first day of school, I used that as a jumping off point for a planned-but-masquerading-as-spontaneous conversation about how we all *learn* and *show our learning* differently. I would start by noticing and complimenting all of the *Mary Janes*, *Stan Smiths*, and *Chuck Taylors* that walked into room 207 that morning.

> *Ooh I love those shoes! Did you pick them out, or did someone else surprise you with them? I love the colors and the tie-dyed laces. Oh and look at yours! I bet you picked out those awesome sneakers. Are they comfortable, or do you need to get used to them for a few days?*

Then I'd segue into how I considered my job as a teacher to be very similar to that of a shoe salesperson. This never failed to get confused looks which I loved because it meant that I had their attention...

> *In our classroom, it is my job to help you learn by providing lessons that fit, are comfortable, and that you like—just like your shoes. No two people in here have the exact same shoes in the exact same size and color, right? Here in our room, it will be the same thing. There will be many ways to learn what fourth and fifth graders need to learn. Just like when you tried on your shoes, you can try on the different styles and strategies I will provide and see if they are comfortable for you. Sometimes you might have to say, "Mrs. Panara, I don't think this fits." And that is okay—it is your right to say it and my job to fix it. Like shoes, I'll just pull a different "pair" off the shelf, and we'll try something new. But sometimes I might say to you, "Walk a little longer in this pair, break them in a little more, and then we'll decide," or "I think you've outgrown these; we're going to try something new." I am going to ask that you work hard, try your best, and give each lesson/strategy a fair shot. That is a deal that we are going to make with each other this year. But I want you to understand, right here on day one, that there is more than one way to do it right. There is more than one way to gain skills and learn information, and there is also more than*

one way to demonstrate to me that you've got it. Fair isn't "everyone gets the same thing." Fair is "everyone gets what they need and what fits them best."

And, year after year, I'd watch a room full of little shoulders that had been situated way up by little earlobes fall to a relaxed position. The collective exhale signaled to me that we were on our way.

There is something so freeing in letting go of the *exclusivity of true* and the *singularity of correct*. Hanging on to those faulty notions is just so limiting. You are an evolving, complex, and beautifully unique person; you don't have to box yourself into something quite so *one size fits all*. Retain your right to decide for *yourself* what is right and valid. Like the Dalai Lama and Edie Brickell remind us, look to your values and listen to your heart. Besides, there is nothing wrong with thinking something is true or correct and then having life show you otherwise. Those epiphanies serve a guiding purpose, one that can direct you to the road on which you're supposed to be.

Takeaway Three

FINDING YOUR PEOPLE

> *"A friend is someone who gives you total freedom to be yourself."* —Jim Morrison

Lucy and Ethel. Chandler and Joey. Harry, Ron and Hermione. Girls who share traveling pants. I think most people would agree that one of life's greatest gifts is that of a true friend. Someone to laugh with. Someone who will gently tell you a hard truth. Someone who will support you when you're at the end of your rope. If that last one makes you think of the final scene in *It's A Wonderful Life*, I'm right there with you. Friends are an essential component of a life well lived, and not just because they'll chip in when you need to come up with $8000 because your Uncle Billy wasn't paying attention and you have a bank examiner breathing down your neck. (I don't think I'll ever be able to watch that final scene with a dry eye; if you haven't seen it, I *highly* suggest adding it to your holiday movie lineup.)

The search for people with whom to connect is part of being human. We all do it. It is the stuff of song lyrics, yearbook quotes, and fortune cookie advice. Finding friendships is a life-long swinging pendulum of struggle and success. But probably more struggle, if I'm being honest, because *a lot* goes into finding and maintaining a healthy friendship. First, there are some permanent marker essentials: *opportunity*, *compatibility*, and *shared expectations*. In other words, you have to meet, like each other, and both want to have a friendship. This is the minimum. Then comes all the pencil stuff... Do you have complementary needs? Similar boundaries? What are you willing to overlook in this flawed human friend? What are you willing to concede of yourself? The questions will evolve, and the answers will change, so don't be surprised when there are some erasures. They just come with the territory.

Hedge Alert

I can only tell the story of how I came to find my own people. That is the only story I have. My experiences as a white, female, suburban, middle-class New Yorker who grew up in the 1980s and early 1990s. You and I may have overlap there; we may not. But, I can assure you that, like yours, mine is a road complete with friendship bumps and lessons learned. I don't maintain that these lessons are 100% universal, or even complete for that matter. You and I both have people we've yet to meet who will become treasured friends. We'll also say goodbye to a few with whom we pictured ourselves growing old and gray. Remember, we are writing the story of our lives in pencil, but so is everyone else. We all have a Pink Pearl in our pocket, making us both powerful and powerless at the very same time.

Survival and Proximity

As with most topics regarding happiness, I tend to start collecting my thoughts by looking at the experiences of children. You've probably noticed that. For me, it is helpful to "start where you start," and we all started as babies receiving at least some level of care from adults. Our very survival depended on it. So, given that you are here today, holding this book, I am going to say that you had at least one responsible caregiver as a baby. Your first people. As babies, we are biologically wired to do whatever we can to keep our people close. I can distinctly remember passing off six-month-old Natalie to my sweet, gentle

Gramma Rene and Natalie, six months old, Christmas 2009

mother-in-law. Natalie was happy with this until I walked out of sight. Then she was very *not* happy with it[9]

I'm guessing from the time you could sit up (and likely before that), your caregivers plunked you down next to another child and said, "This is your friend." Not really having a say in the matter, you probably thought, "Okay, she seems fine, but she cannot have my Cheerios, blankie, rubber giraffe, or Mommy." As long as said friend didn't take your stuff, you were probably fine with the adjacent placement. For babies and toddlers, this seems to be the big friendship criteria: *do not take what is mine or what I have decided is mine.* But as long as that rule was upheld, proximity equaled friendship. Your friends were probably the children of your parents' friends, your neighbors, and possibly the kids you met *that day* at the playground.[10] It almost didn't

---

9   The record must reflect that Gramma Rene, pronounced Reen as in Irene, quickly became one of Natalie's people, too.

10   Shout out to Amy Feingold, Adam Molberger, and Marni Sussman. Glad to have been plunked down beside you.

matter if you liked these peers or not—this was it. This was the entire applicant pool. They were convenient for your adults, they were right there in front of you, and, frankly, you didn't have the mobility or means to look elsewhere.

Newly able to show your age with *ALL* the fingers on one hand (thank you very much), you now head off to school. Proximity still played a role in your ability to find friends, but you were certainly able to cast a wider net. The criteria remained a little self-serving (your BFF for the day was probably the kid who shared his Cool Ranch Doritos with you at snack, especially if your mom always packed you raisins), but you are no longer seeking connections just to survive. You discover that friendships bring joy. Your friends probably changed a little during this time, depending on who was in your class that year, but I'm sure that you can look back on your elementary school days and remember the kids with whom you were most happy palling around.[11] Although I could not have articulated it at the time, my people were those kids who weren't trying to be older than we were. Translation: we could be silly together. We were not trying to uphold some sort of image. I don't think that even *occurred* to us. And as such, an important friendship ingredient revealed itself: accepting, enjoying, and joining in on my silly. *Too-cool eye rollers* need not apply.

Independence and Identity

Then came middle school. Ohhhh middle school—the almost-universal bumpy road. The awkward center of a Venn diagram mapping the attributes of little kids and young adults. The nobody-is-just-one-thing existence when it was *makeup* by day and *stuffed animal hugging* by night. Remember how baby Natalie cried when I walked out of the room? Now, in middle school herself, I think she'd cry if I stayed in it. But I get it; the entire early-teenage ordeal

---

11   Here's to Bethany Pomes Pisani and Laurie Focacci: my most favorite elementary
      school pals.

is, in my opinion, a giant experiment in finding your *independence* and *identity*.

With emotions running high and moods changing hourly, it stands to reason that your middle school friendships were somewhat rocky and fleeting. How could they not be? Adolescence brings with it the fear of being shunned for being yourself. *If I show everyone who I really am, I will be judged, and I will be rejected.* That said, these friendships were of utmost importance at the time because they signaled to the world that you "fit in." Are you picking up on the irony here? It's as if you were suddenly cast in the role of "trendy confident tween," so if you acted like your regular old self, you were going off-script. For these reasons, *come-as-you-are, elementary school Melissa* now felt the need to impress the aforementioned *too-cool eye rollers*. I won't include any names from my past, but I am sure you can think of a few from yours.

Thankfully for me, it wasn't this way for the entirety of my middle school experience. *Silly* still had a place in my social life, and there is video proof. In seventh grade, my friend Julie and I decided to record a cooking show in my kitchen called *Chow Down with Maude and Rhoda*. I named myself Rhoda because I loved Valerie Harper on reruns of *The Mary Tyler Moore Show*. I have no idea why Julie called herself Maude, but I have to say, it really worked. We had my *totally-up-for-this* dad videotape us making pancakes while we wore feather barrettes and spoke in Southern accents. Don't waste any time trying to make sense of it—there's none to be made. We were twelve years old, giddy, and had access to a cameraman. That's it. In the middle of the show, the phone rang, so I'm on tape breaking character, taking a message for my sister, then jumping right back in. That made it all the better. So I consider myself lucky because middle school was not the full-on nightmare for me that it is for so many people. However, it certainly wasn't bumpless. I can definitely remember having to think about "who to be" in different social situations, often concluding that the *actual Melissa* was not nearly good enough. And that was pretty soul-sucking. No wonder I was a jerk to my mom. Sorry, Mom. I get it now.

Presumably grateful to be looking at middle school in the rearview mirror, you now head to high school. For me, the year was 1990, and I remember feeling like I had hit the big time. Independence kicks into a higher gear; it was a time of drivers' licenses and first jobs. You probably made dinner or did laundry for the first time. You gained some experience allocating your time among schoolwork, afterschool commitments, and time with friends. And it was probably up to you to make adjustments if one thing was pulling too much time from another. Being a responsible kid, those things came pretty naturally to me. *Identity*, however, was the area that needed my attention: I had to find the path back to being the genuine me. Here's how that went: as freshmen, my friends and I were what I'd call popular-adjacent. We were friendly with the "cool kids," walked to and from class together, went to their parties at the beach, knew some of their inside jokes, etc... but all at a price.[12]

The time and energy that went into maintaining this popular-adjacent status was crazy. We had to be vigilant—no days off, no going off-script. Not to mention having to lie and break rules in order to be seen at the right places. I hated that. But as a friend group since middle school, together we tried it on for size. And among us, there were varying levels of comfort with it all. Me? You guessed it: *not at all comfortable but totally faking it to stay socially afloat.* If the comfort scale was one to ten, I was a big ol' zero. A zero who was flat-out exhausted from trying to fit the nebulous, just-out-of-reach social expectation of the in-crowd. Were these people actually my friends? What exactly was I chasing here? Was happiness at the other end of this chase? Was I close to the end? Did it even *have* an end? All

---

12   I remember someone telling me, as a party newbie, a rule called "Cop, Drop, and Run". So, obviously, if I saw a police officer, I was to drop my cup and run. Silly Melissa immediately thought how funny it would be if someone got confused and did stop, drop and roll instead. Everyone else is running away, leaving one idiot rolling around on the sand. But of course I didn't say this to anyone. What I also didn't say was, "Run where, exactly? We're on a beach with barriers and backyards on each side, so unless we're all swimming to Connecticut, don't we basically have to run toward the police officer? Listen, you seem great, and thanks for the help, but I don't think I'm cut out for this."

I knew for sure is that I was way too young to be this tired and that I was none the happier for my efforts.

Eventual Epiphany

Something happens when you hit your limit. I don't know what it is, but something visceral happens and you hear yourself say "Oh FORGET it, I'm OUT!" (Definitely with harsher wording, but I'm trying to keep it family friendly here). In this particular situation, it was probably a combination of maturing and realizing that I had other viable options. Friends in my classes, people in my clubs and other activities, kids I found funny or interesting. There were over 450 kids in my class for crying out loud; I was literally surrounded by friend potential. I just needed to *erase* some things and *rewrite* some things. And it wasn't that I didn't like my friends anymore (I *still* like these people thirty years later). I never wanted to Pink Pearl *them*, I just wanted off the merry-go-round. They seemed happy to keep riding, and that was fine.

But, thanks to my mid-high school epiphany, my bottom line finally came into focus: I wanted to be with people who wanted to be with me. The authentic me. The silly, oldies-and-show-tunes-loving, rule-following, tradition-starting, always-dancing, sings-off-key, extroverted-but-sentimental Melissa. For the first time since seventh grade, I stopped hiding her. I stopped censoring her. I just returned to *being* her, and the universe rewarded me for it. The *knowing* was difficult, but the *doing* was easy because being yourself takes literally no effort.[13] If you don't stand in your own way, it just happens. Perhaps our early teenage years are designed to deliver this very lesson; they take us away from the purest version of ourselves, bump and jostle us around, and bring us to the realization that being ourselves is the only way to get to a smoother road. A more comfortable road. And, if you are as lucky as me, a road along which you'll find a permanent-marker-friend-for-life like Pam Clark. We were

---

13   More on the knowing-doing gap in the next chapter.

(Top) Pam and me in 1993. (Middle) Pam and me in 2022. (Bottom) This is a mug I gave Pam when we were somewhere in our thirties. Looking at this picture, I can hear her laughing. If you have a friend like this, stop reading for a minute and send them a text.

always too busy laughing and goofing off for sixteen-year-old me to realize that I had stopped thinking about who to be. I didn't need to anymore.

Change on the Horizon

From this point on, high school flew. Being truly happy will do that—move your life along at a rapid pace. Before I knew it, my friends and I were off to college, going in our separate directions. This was tough because I finally loved my social life just as it was; I didn't want anything to change. But since my high school didn't have a thirteenth grade, I had to find my bravery (and my pencil) and write my next chapter. Thankfully, a few good things were in place for me: I had had recent success finding my people, dorms filled with incoming freshmen are fertile ground for finding even more, and, best of all, residence life gave me Kara Seeley for a roommate. I didn't yet know it, but I hit the lottery that day.

Those first few weeks at college were tough, I'm not going to lie. I was 360 miles from home, and I felt every last one of them. I missed my people so much—it was a minor miracle that I didn't just start walking home. Kara, on the other hand, grew up twenty minutes away from campus, and as such, was much closer to her comfort zone.[14] So close, in fact, her parents told her she couldn't go home for at least a month. From what I recall, she was more than fine with that. I very much wanted to show Kara the authentic me, especially because I sensed a lot of overlap, but because nothing around me felt familiar or comfortable, I couldn't find her. That first week at school, the silly, oldies-and-show-tunes-loving, rule-following, tradition-starting, always-dancing, sings-off-key, extroverted-but-sentimental Melissa was nowhere to be found.

This was not a problem for Kara; I think she understood what a jump in cold water this was for me and that my sadness would likely

---

14   I used to tell Kara that she could Pogo-stick to her home faster than I could drive to mine, and it was probably true.

be temporary. With intuition and empathy far beyond her seventeen years, she gave me the benefit of the doubt. She chose to see something worth redeeming in the sad-sack on the bed across the room. And, as if she couldn't stop it if she tried, she showed me *her* authentic self. Her hilarious, encouraging, country-music-loving, soccer-playing, chats-up-literally-everyone, confident-but-self-deprecating, works-hard-plays-hard, just-as-silly-as-me self. And it got me through. It took virtually no time to see, with permanent-marker-level confidence, that I had found another one of my people.

Reasons and Seasons

Known by the portmanteau *Karamel*, the two of us easily found people to hang out with those first days and weeks of college. (I wasn't sad 24/7, just to clarify). Once again, friend potential was literally everywhere. Looking back, the whole scenario is surprisingly reminiscent of how we "made friends" as babies. This time, though, we were plunked down in a dorm next to two hundred-plus undergrads. And like before (at least initially), proximity equaled friendship. As that first semester continued, some of those first connections fell away because they were *friends for a reason*: we were all acclimating to living away from home, we were assigned to the same dorm, and we all wanted to meet new people. There is nothing wrong with that. *Friends for a reason* is a totally legitimate category of friends; it serves a specific and real purpose. It just comes with a shelf life. When these friendships ended, I didn't feel hurt. Truthfully, I barely noticed.

Of the friends that remained and the new ones we found, most would land in the next category: *Friends for a season*. These are people with whom I had an absolute blast,[15] but our friendships ultimately existed inside those four years of college. Because that is where we had all of those permanent marker minimums: *opportunity, compatibility,* and *shared expectations*. In addition, we had a season's worth of

---

15   Absolute blast memories: 14,000 of them, give or take. Shout out to my college friends from any category. See Appendix for more.

Kara and me silly
then, silly now.

sustained proximity and *overlapping purpose*. Everything about our friendships was real, but the context was the glue. Though we may have wanted to, we couldn't extend the season much further. Sure, there were post-graduation New Year's Eve parties, Memorial Day pig roasts, and eventually a lot of weddings. But, ultimately, time showed us that we really needed that *proximity* and *overlap of purpose* to keep the train moving. The momentum of life was pushing us all forward and in different directions, and everyone needed to invest in writing the next chapter of our lives.

With my own brand of optimistic innocence and naivete, I fought against this. But when my efforts started to become one-sided, I had to face what was happening. Life can only move forward, and I was a friend from a time that had passed. *It wasn't personal; it was seasonal.* Every now and then I reach out to one of these college (or high school) friends, just to say hello or catch up a little. Because I still care about them. But it is a small group because, typically, it's only me sustaining the connection. I am aware of this, but it makes me happy, so I choose to do it anyway.

If you are feeling sad for me, you don't have to because I am about to get to the best part. *Friends for life.*[16] These are the friends that started out in another group but for reasons beyond what words can

---

16   By the way, I cannot claim to have originated the reason/season/life friend categories. Sometimes Eleanor Roosevelt gets credit, sometimes it's someone named Brian A. "Drew" Chalker, but never Melissa Panara. Just wanted to be clear on that.

fully capture, there is mutual interest and a shared effort to keep it all going. Besides Kara Seeley Mathis, college gifted me Carolyn (Stojo) Stojanovich Capozzi and Francine Ferrantelli John as ride-or-die lifers. My forever and ever people. More on lifers below.

Real World Time

Singer-songwriter and low-level bad boy John Mayer got it wrong; there IS such a thing as the real world, and it can be very tricky to find your people out here. I'm still in the midst of writing the "Fine, Fine, I'll Be An Adult" chapter of my life, but I can offer you a few highlights from the content thus far.

As an adult, I have found that *friends for a reason* can be found around just about every corner. Neighbors, co-workers, people at PTA meetings and over-thirty pickup soccer games (known as "old man soccer" in the Panara family)—these are the people who *happen* to be in the same place as you and with whom you click. These connections are convenient and largely casual but still contribute to a happy life;

Our Ruby, eleven months old, April 2021

they are important. A few months ago, while walking our dog, I ran into our neighbor, John. He is someone I had come to know more so from overlap at Cub Scouts and school events than from living a few streets apart. We hadn't talked in a while because our kids have grown past the activities that originally linked us. But we stopped to chat a bit, and it turns out that we each had some pretty significant (and not awesome) news to share in the family update department. Our concern for each other was genuine, so a new reason was born. A few days later, I sent him a message just to say I was glad we talked and if he needed a sympathetic ear, he could reach out. He reiterated his concern for me and asked to be kept in the loop. I left that exchange reminded that the world is full of good people, and small interactions can yield heartwarming results. *Friends for a reason* matter.

Just like in college, some of these same-place-as-me folks have crossed over into the realm of *friends for a season* (aka my actual, current friends). There is *proximity, compatibility,* and *shared expectations.* But there is also *reciprocal effort,* a hugely important feature; I'm not the only one keeping this train moving. If Mike and I were to throw a New Year's Eve party, these would be the people on our guest list. And, I'll mark the calendar, because we'll be spending Memorial Day at their pig roast. If you are one of these friends, I am going to reach out to find a time to meet for coffee, dinner, or to catch a show of some kind. Maybe a pub trivia night or backyard bonfire. And—fair warning—it is likely that I'm going to try to talk you into joining me for karaoke. (Seriously, just try it. I'm an awful singer, but I've discovered it is all in the song choice. Try *Bust A Move* by Young MC. You *know* you know all the words...)

I'm comfortable categorizing these seasonal friends as "my people" because they truly are my friends. However, it remains to be seen if any of these pig-roasters and karaoke-avoiders will be added to the *friends for life* category. Truth be told, it is probably too early to tell. I have some pencil mark predictions, but I have to see if those permanent marker prerequisites have staying power. The passing of time does matter here. Will there be sustained, mutual interest and effort beyond the season we're sharing? Will something cut our season short? Since my crystal ball is in the shop, I'll just bide my time and enjoy the ride. My heart will tell me everything I need to know.

Encouraging a Reasonal[17] to Seasonal Upgrade

About five years ago, I felt I was in a socialization slump. I wanted some more *friend time* on my calendar, so I decided to do something a little out of my comfort zone. I got to thinking that perhaps there was some untapped friend potential in my *friends for a reason* group, so I decided to email some of them. Using the blind carbon copy option (BCC) so the recipient list would be hidden, I wrote something to the effect of *Hey, I noticed we have a lot of laughs when we're together and thought maybe you'd be interested in hanging out a little more...* It was a little bit of a risk, but I had decided it was one worth taking.

Of the six people I emailed, I got only two replies. One friend expressed enthusiasm and gratitude, and it felt amazing. We were on the same page. Game on! The other responded with one sentence: "Thanks, but I'm just super busy right now." Ouch. I was not prepared for a flat-out rejection. My inner twelve-year-old said, "You SEE! THIS is why you don't go off-script!" In fairness, I did ask the question, and she held up her end of the bargain with a response. Twelve- and forty-one-year-old me felt the sting, but then I took the perspective that it wasn't personal. Perhaps she really WAS super busy; I didn't know her well enough to say that she wasn't. Maybe she had passed her manageable friend quota. Maybe she was running from the law and sensed my inner Encyclopedia Brown would put all the pieces together. Who knows? My point is sometimes you have to be vulnerable and take a chance. Nothing ventured, nothing gained. I got one strengthened friendship as a result of my little email venture, and one is not zero. Plus, my inner *sixteen-year-old* reminded me that I didn't really want to be with people who didn't want to be

---

17   Let's just pretend this is a real word.

with *me* anyway. This callback to a decades-old epiphany reminded me of something important: friends worth having valued *my* friendship as well.

Okay, just one more tiny anecdote... but, for variety, I'll present it in the form of a short sketch. Note from the director: Do it justice and imagine all the facial expressions.

> *Me: (Said something mildly snarky but in a low voice)*
>
> *Reasonal friend within earshot: (Looks at me and smiles)*
>
> *Me: I said that out loud, didn't I? As you get to know me, you may notice I say things aloud that should probably stay in my head.*
>
> *Still smiling reasonal friend: Hey, that will only earn you points with me.*
>
> *Me: (translates that as "I'm good with real. Come as you are.") (thinks: Hmmm, there's some good friend potential here...)*
>
> *Roll credits. Throw roses.*

My Running List of Takeaways

Get comfy, friends, because I have a lot of thoughts here. If you need to refill your water or get another blanket, now's the time.

Annnnd we're back.

Did you know that the single best predictor of our psychological health, well-being, physical health, and even how long we live, is the number and the quality of close friends that we have? Not hours of REM sleep, not regular exercise, not matcha-turmeric-bone broth smoothies. Thank God for small miracles.

Fitting in versus Belonging

Going back to middle school for a minute (I won't subject you to more than that, I promise), remember the irony of playing a part in order to fit in? We didn't want to show our potential friends our authentic selves in an attempt to avoid rejection. This is a stumbling block that has the potential to be a life-changing stepping stone. Here's why: there is a big difference between "fitting in" and "belonging."

Fitting in is going with the flow of someone else's expectations or definitions. Most anyone can *fit in* if they play the part. However, fitting in requires you to think about who to be and to stay on-script. Is that really sustainable? Is what you're gaining *real* and worth the effort? I can't answer for you, but I will say this: the real you is worth being and worth knowing. Hand me a Sharpie so I can write that down for you.

Belonging is much simpler because all you have to do is be yourself. If there is true belonging, your people will allow you to bring ALL of yourself into the room. You get to be the flawed person you are. You can mess up and not be kicked out. You can have short-comings without being defined by them... because nobody is just one thing. When you belong, there are no nebulous requirements, no term limits, no fine print. It's about who you are, not what you are trying to portray. When friends earn the *for life* distinction (or bestow it on you), it happens because there is a mutual sense of belonging.

And if you don't belong where you're trying to be, that is okay too. Forcing that fit is a recipe for discomfort and anxiety. The moment of realization and rejection hurts, I know. It is real pain. But once the sting subsides, there is a kindness underneath—it is the universe telling you there is something better out there for you. Somewhere you truly belong and where your worth will be celebrated. Keep trying to find it. Keep looking. It is worth the vulnerability and effort. There's someone out there looking for you, too.

Quality and Quantity

When thinking about your people, both quality and quantity matter. Here's how I break it down: Reasonal friends—the list is long but the connection is weak. Seasonal friends—the list is shorter but the bonds are more substantial. Lifers: the list is shorter still but each connection is one you can't imagine your life without.

Your list might be different, but I have a few criteria that categorize a friend as a lifer:

- When I look *forward to* or *back on* our time together, I feel both comfortable and confident.
- They seek time or connection with me; I don't always have to be the one reaching out. We prioritize each other. That said, time can pass, and we always pick up right where we left off.
- We've weathered and survived at least some bumps along the way (read: they've forgiven me when I've messed up).
- I feel like one of a select few rather than one of a stadium's worth of best friends. "Special" kind of goes out the window at that point.

Fran (left) and Stojo (right) check everything on my list.

Friends in Unexpected Places

When you are a child, your friends are other children because, with very few exceptions, anything else would be, well, creepy. But as you get older, age matters less. It becomes about common ground and true connection—which is ageless. I consider myself truly blessed to have had such a friend in Grace Dominge Taylor.

In high school, Pam and I were part of a club called Grandfriends. It worked like this: a pair of students got matched up with a senior citizen in our community for the purpose of forging a friendship. Typically, these were people who lived alone and could benefit from the companionship. The minimum requirement was to connect with your Grandfriend every other week: once by phone, once in person. Pam and I hit the jackpot when we got matched up with Grace Taylor. We could not have loved her more—our Amazing Grace.

Pam, Grace, and me on the day of the Senior Prom, June 1994.

Over cookies and "black cows" on her little balcony, Grace asked us about our classes and our families. She looked at the photo albums and mementos that we brought along to share. In turn, Grace showed us her original paintings, shared *her* photo albums, and told us story after story from her very full life. She was a proud alumna of Douglass College, which was the women's college at Rutgers University. She also earned an "advanced degree" (as she called it) from Columbia University. Grace was a retired high school art teacher, as well as an artist and sculptor in her own right. She married Harry Taylor, whom she always referred to as *Harry Taylor*, well into adulthood and was happy to love his children and grandchildren as her own. By the time we met her at age 84, Harry Taylor had passed on, and Grace was living alone in their Scudder Avenue home. I mention this because I remember being fascinated by one of her many "town history" stories: she explained to Pam and me that their house was situated right there, in that very spot, even before Scudder Avenue existed. In those days, her front yard was actually her backyard and her address was Main Street.

As if I were a college kid talking about vehicles being *cars* or *trucks*, I could talk about Grace Taylor for years on end. I won't... but, in loving tribute to one of the best people I will ever know, I am going to share a little bit more.

- Every New Years Day, Grace would hold an open house party which I attended several times. The wide-range of guests, many of whom did not know each other, was very much reflective of a host who made friends wherever she went.
- Noticing a boat named *Amazing Grace* in her neighbor's backyard, I pointed out the coincidence. Turns out it was not a coincidence at all. Grace told us a story about how she happened to inherit the boat and decided to give it to her sea-loving young neighbor, no strings attached.
- When Pam and I went to college, Grace gave us two things: a coffee mug filled with quarters for the coin-operated washers and dryers in our dorms, and a chalkboard for our doors so people could leave us messages. Twenty-nine years later, I still have and use my mug. The chalkboard, which came with a hand-written message too precious to erase, hangs inside my closet above the door so it will never be accidentally erased.

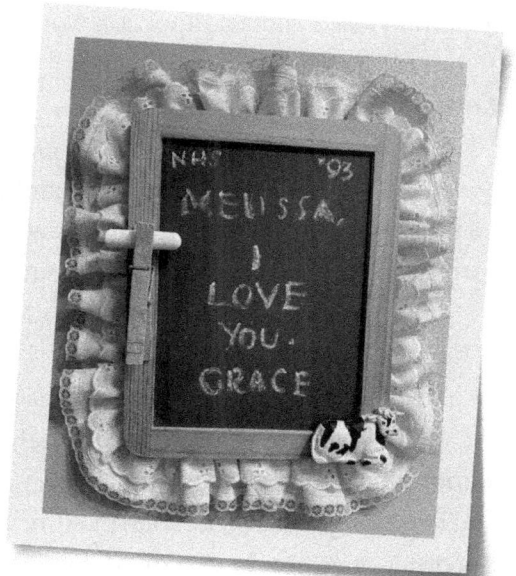

- When Mike and I got married in 2002, we invited Grace to our wedding. She was ninety-four years old at the time, and her vision had declined so much, so she could not attend. She did, though, send us a check with a note that read: *Buy something nice, and then call me to congratulate me on my good taste.*

- When Michael was born in 2007, I called Grace to let her know I had become a mom. I remember her saying that she was so happy *for Michael* because he was going to have "a wonderful mother." Grace passed away a few months later, and due to the nursing-my-newborn-every-two-hours thing, I could not travel and attend her funeral, which hurts my heart to this day.

Even though Grace and I were sixty-eight years apart in age, we had a true connection. She is a lifer with whom I shared a fifteen-year friendship. I think about her wit, her insights, and her optimism all the time; they have become a part of me. And it all started because we shared a love of our little seaside town and drinks made of ice cream and root beer. But over time and even distance, we found in each other a kindred spirit and a connection worth holding on to.

Letting Go

This one can be emotional, but I don't think there's any getting around it. Not all friendships are meant to last. Sometimes you'll be the *let-go-ee*, and your emotions will likely be in the sadness, confusion, and hurt by rejection category.

Sometimes you'll be the *let-go-er*, and the emotions might be some combination of guilt and relief. Though some endings can be abrupt and dramatic, I think most are more of a slow fade into the ether. Regardless, I have found that the road tends to be a lot smoother when you are in agreement with the person from whom you're parting. However, if one person wants things to keep going and the other does not, buckle up; the smooth road is going to become a bit bumpier.

In my experience, friendships wane for a few reasons. Boundaries are ignored, trust is broken, or there just isn't a mutual investment in the relationship. I have had friendships lapse for all of these reasons. The most common for me has been the mutual investment one.

Maybe in the past, I would have put an endless amount of effort in keeping a friendship going, but, frankly, I'm over that. I put in a good amount of effort in the beginning, but, if in the short term, it isn't reciprocated with a similar enthusiasm, it's time to let things lie. I am not going to chase someone who doesn't want to be caught. I like to think of it showing my inner self-respect on the outside. I have confidence that I am good at being a friend; I am worth someone's effort. However, if someone doesn't see that or match up with my brand of friendship, well, then it just allows me more time with the people who do.

Sometimes the following happens: I run into someone out in the world with whom I've socialized in the past. She says, "We should get together! It's been too long! Text me and let me know when you're free." If this happens once, I'm happy to assume it is a good-faith offer. But if it happens more than once, I've come to see it as the person giving me an assignment. "I'm willing to hang out with you if you do the work, and if it doesn't end up happening, it is on you." Okay, maybe this is on the harsh side of possible interpretations, but it has happened enough for me to have a little chip on my shoulder regarding the veiled message of *You won't be hearing from ME, oh no no no, but we can hang out if YOU want to try getting on my calendar.* Readers, I'm trying my best in this book to offer *possibilities to consider* rather than *protocols to follow*, but I think I am going to break my own rule on this one. Don't do this to people. It is like saying, "You're not worth my effort." And how much effort is it, exactly? A ten-word text? *Want to meet for coffee Saturday morning at the Junction?* If someone can't do that for you, maybe it's fine if you don't meet up. Show your self-respect on the outside; you deserve more than that.

I'm sure you've heard this one before: there are many fish in the sea. No argument here—this is both quantifiably and metaphorically true. Usually, it refers to finding a significant other, but it applies to friendships, too. Fishing has always been one of my dad's favorite pastimes. Off the dock, off a boat, in waders—all of it. It was one of the ways he bonded with his own dad, and it was his plan to bond with my sister and me in the very same way. One giant clue to that end was the fact that he owned a book called *Teaching Your Children To Fish*. It was a big, green, hardbound tome, and for my entire childhood, it lived on top of the roll-top desk in our den. Google afforded me a picture of the cover and the fact that it is *243 pages*. For real? It took the author *243 pages* to explain this? Anyway, fishing with Tara and me, as little girls, was definitely the fiasco you are imagining. I remember crying because I didn't want to hurt the worms or see a fish with a hook in its mouth. I remember *Tara* crying because she was terrified of being in a boat on choppy water and because every part of the experience smelled absolutely disgusting. Just a guess that there was nothing in the 243 pages that could remedy *all that*. Sorry, Dad—I am sure this was not the watercolor image in your head when you bought the big green book. At least now you have the grandkids—and thankfully, because they are on board, Tara and I are off the hook. (Was that *two more* fishing metaphors? They really are *everywhere*.)

But my dad will be happy that I did learn some important lessons from the years (and years) of fishing together. You have to cast over and over again just for the *chance* of catching a fish. You cast, you wait, you watch the bobber to see if it gets tugged under. Sometimes it does, but most of the time you're reeling back in and trying again. I feel like I've fished enough to say that the entire pastime is, essentially, "trying again." And even when you catch a fish, sometimes it isn't right. It is too small; you have to set it free so it can grow—maybe you'll catch that exact fish again next year when it is ready. (*Wait, we're doing this again next year?*) Ultimately, after what feels like a million casts, you catch a keeper. I am sure you are picking up what I am putting down here. But the part I want to highlight is this: when you let go of a friendship, try not to think of it as "throwing them back." That feels as harsh as "erasing" someone. If you think of it as "letting them swim away," giving them a chance to grow/experience/evolve, then maybe someday you'll catch them again. But right now, something isn't right, and that is okay. Maybe they'll "swim back"

(Top) Michael (or possibly toddler Joe Torre) driving Poppy's boat. (Middle and bottom) Michael and Natalie fishing with Poppy. Not pictured: my sister Tara and I, somewhere else, getting pedicures.

when the circumstances are better. But if they don't, that is also fine; they are out there *finding their people.* And so are you. We all deserve that freedom. Hanging on to them does a disservice to both of you... AND to the people you are *not* meeting by extending this friendship beyond its sell-by date.

The Bottom Line

To find your real people, the people worth having you, here it is... my permanent marker, core belief:

1. Your part: Put yourself out there, and be the real you. Repeat as necessary.
2. Their part: Showing you that you are a priority and welcoming all of you into the room. Don't settle for anything less.

Takeaway Four

CHOOSING
YOUR PERSPECTIVE

> *"Bees can sting, and that is bad. But they also make honey, which is really good. I like to think about them making honey."* —Natalie Panara, age seven

I can sum up this chapter with the following sentence. Don't underestimate the power of your perspective. Regardless of what you're looking at, *how* you choose to look at it is paramount.

You don't have to break it to me gently; I know that I am not the first person to suggest such a thing. Everyone from Greek philosophers to *Peanuts* characters has said some version of "Try looking at it differently; maybe you'll see the good." So even though the following isn't exactly groundbreaking content, I'm including it because I've found that choosing a perspective is a key piece of the happiness puzzle. In fact, it is often a major player in our decision to either stick with Plan A or move on to Plan B. What's more, what we choose to focus on can lead us to that post-bump takeaway from which we make decisions. Best of all, our perspective is written in pencil. We can rethink, erase, and rewrite it whenever we choose. It's when using our flexible brain can literally change the course of our lives.

The View from Here

Imagine that you are playing a guessing game with a five-year-old boy. You tell him you are thinking of something *blue, green,* and *tiny.* Even with a zillion[18] guesses, he might never guess Earth. You could explain that Earth IS tiny compared to the Sun or Jupiter, but your little friend might respond with, "Nooo! Earth is huge! My whole HOUSE fits on Earth!" Technically, he's not wrong; I am quite certain that his entire house is, in fact, *on Earth.* He can't yet appreciate that size is relative, not absolute. Developmentally, young children have limited abilities in perspective taking. They are not *choosing* to look from a singular point of view; this is just how their young minds work. They can't "find" the good because they are not wired to stop and consider other possibilities; they are uber-confident in their conclusions and motivated to tell you ALL about them. (This is one of the many reasons why I love working in a K-2 school. *Tell me all about it, kids.*)

Early Role Models

Maturity brings with it the ability to consider a single thing in multiple ways. As growing kids, we start to notice others modeling this before we give it a try ourselves. For me, one of these early role models was my dad—a glass-half-full guy if ever there was one. For years, my sister Tara and I have described him as *jolly,* and he is the source of countless "find the good" stories. Here's a favorite: Back in the days before caller ID, quite literally anyone could be on the other end of a ringing phone. Kind of unnerving, right? Not to our dad... *ohhh* no; the man could talk to a wrong number for an hour. Dad would answer the phone with his signature, slightly-too-loud *HELLO,* and if it was followed by a period of silence, we'd know that he was probably listening to the pitch of a telemarketer. Once it was his turn

---

18   A real number to the majority of five-year-olds

to talk, he'd say something like, "You know you make a really good point about the dust that gets trapped in wall-to-wall carpeting; isn't that true! My daughter Melissa does have allergies. Our vacuum is relatively new, though, Marty, and we're saving to put two kids through college. But keep up that enthusiasm—you're going to get the next one! Okay, okay, you bet! So long!"[19] Our mom got so sick of these telemarketer pep-talks, which was funny in its own right, but Tara and I loved them. To our dad, this person was someone's son. He was just doing his job like everyone else. And let's be honest. It probably wasn't Marty's childhood dream to grow up and become a telemarketer so he could bug people during the dinner hour. But to our dad, it didn't cost anything to throw a little positivity his way. He knew Marty was probably yelled at and hung up on multiple times every day. Dad took what most people found to be an annoying situation, and he found the good. In this case, he provided it. And Tara and I were listening and learning.

Do As I Say...

Now, I will admit that even as an adult, this is an area of life where I often fall into the knowing-doing gap.[20] Having a cup of regular coffee at 2:00 pm is a good example; I know it is going to keep me up that night, but I want it right now, so I drink it anyway. "Now" Melissa is quite content, but "wide awake at midnight" Melissa is going to be so mad at her. The knowing-doing gap also comes into play when it is something I *don't* do even though I know I should—the knowing-*not*-doing gap, if you will. Anyone who has ever joined a gym in January is likely to be with me on this one. *It's a great deal right now, and of course I am going to go to the gym three times a week starting on January 2nd because I know it is healthy, so that is what I'll do.* Nope. So, even though I know I should look at any given situation in more than one way to find the good, a lot of the time I just don't do

---

19   "You bet" and "So long" - Two classic sign-off phrases for my dad. I am almost positive he considers them to be mandatory.

20   Check out the book by Jeffrey Pfeffer and Robert Sutton, Harvard Business School Press.

it. I could say I'm too busy looking for vegan dinner recipes that will simultaneously please both my teenagers, but I gave up on searching for that unicorn years ago. But to paraphrase my Natalie-pep talk, this is just one more way I'm proving to you that I'm human, but you guys already knew that.

So, here's what I KNOW: Assuming a vantage point other than your own is where empathy comes from. Seeing something from a positive angle is where gratitude comes from. Finding an alternate route is where opportunity comes from. A lot of good can come from *walking over there* and taking another glance. It is completely possible that we are standing in our own blind spot. Now the DOING: This takes practice, but as my kids learned in elementary school, practice makes *progress*. I really liked the early lesson in not expecting effort to result in flawlessness. Good on you, Jefferson Avenue School teachers. Bottom line: Keep at it. Rome wasn't built in a day. However, I like to think that someone on the Roman construction crew said, "*Ottimo lavoro a tutti!* Good job, everyone! We still have a ways to go—but *look* at all we've accomplished since lunch! Gelato for everybody!" I want to be that guy.

And As I Do...Sometimes

Even though I'm still very much a work-in-progress, I do have a story or two to illustrate my growing skills in perspective-taking. Times when I have experienced the life-affirming happiness boost that comes from *acknowledging* the stinger but *enjoying* the honey.

Happiness boost number one: my perspective shift on nursing my newborn babies overnight. Both Michael and Natalie ate every two hours for months on end. Day and night. Every. Two. Hours. Hearing a cry and seeing 2:51 AM on the clock, my initial, exhausted, new mom reaction was "Agaaaain? You're hungry again? Oh come *on*, man, be reasonable! I am soooo tired, and I just fell back to sleep..." Looking over at Mike, all cozy and blissfully unaware, certainly did not help matters. Irrationally, I resented him for not being able to take turns with me and told him repeatedly, "You owe me so big time." I don't know where I heard it or why it occurred to me (Divine intervention? *Today*

Show segment? Parenting books now hidden in the garage?), but I started to see those middle-of-the-night meet-ups for the blessing that they were. In the quiet warmth of my home, I got to hold my sweet, precious miracle and offer a comfort that no one else could... and this novel perspective flooded my heart with a new and overwhelming joy. My baby had come to know that when he cried, I would come. He trusted that completely; it was his one, tiny vantage point: *This lady's got me.* I get teary-eyed just thinking about it. In his own innocent way, he knew he was safe and cared for because, over and over, I was giving him the proof.

I'd also come to realize that these moments were fleeting, and suddenly I wanted to savor what I had previously scorned. My children would always need me, but not in this way for very long. So, as my baby nursed, I closed my eyes and thought about what an honor it is to be someone's mother. I realized that there were mothers and babies all over the world doing this very thing right now. And I thought that maybe it was *me* that owed *Mike* "big time" for getting to enjoy what I now consider to be the closest thing to a perfect moment that life has to offer.

Happiness boost number two: my perspective shift on letting someone go. This one even surprised me. One of the hardest things I've ever been through is the loss of my Nana, Dee Centola, in 2002. She died five months before my wedding, and it broke my heart. When she was dying, hospice nurses came to the house to care for her. If angels on earth exist, I am convinced they come in the form of these end-of-life caregivers. I quickly learned they were actually there to care for *all of us*, and that is exactly what they did. During one of the first visits, a nurse gave my family a poem called "Gone From My Sight" by Henry Van Dyke. The words were simple and comforting, and they offered a perspective I hadn't considered. In the poem, the dying person is compared to a great ship. You are invited to picture yourself standing beside it as it sets sail. Smaller and smaller it becomes as it approaches the horizon and finally disappears out of sight. From our perspective, it is gone. In actuality, though, nothing about the ship has changed;

it is just as big and beautiful and strong as when we stood beside it. *And, just at the moment when someone says, "There, she is gone," there are other eyes watching her coming, and other voices ready to take up the glad shout, "Here she comes!"* Cue the goosebumps. These words helped me to envision my Nana as unchanged (still 5' ¾"—big personality, small packaging), simply leaving one place and arriving at another. My earthly, mortal vantage point was not the only perspective I could take. Even though it crushed me to let her go, I pictured family members I had never met standing along a sunny shoreline cheering her arrival. It softened the pain, made the unbearable just a little more bearable. And even though my grief continues to this day, I love picturing her reunited with her parents, siblings, and the cast of characters from her many stories, including, but not limited to, Mrs. Dangle, her favorite teacher; Alma, her friend that moved to Texas; Ben, her beloved hairdresser (hilarious but true); Dr. Palmieri, podiatrist and former boss; and any number of her Brooklyn or Jersey cousins. Today, in my mind's eye, she is dancing the Peabody with my grandfather while a roaring band plays their favorite song, *It's a Sin to Tell A Lie*. And I picture the day, many years from now, when I see her face come into focus as I sail toward a distant but ever-nearing shoreline.

* * *

Just as choosing our perspective can give us a lift, it can also help us to avoid a let-down. Oftentimes we need to take a second look in order to see a situation for what it *is*, rather than what we want it to be. Try as we might, there are certain things that we just cannot "will into being." When we first had kids, Mike was absolutely flabbergasted by the amount of stuff that babies required. He could not get over it. I will admit, even before he was born, it *did* seem like Michael owned more stuff than we did. As parents-to-be, we were gifted everything that the modern American baby could possibly need. This included a variety of items designed to stimulate or soothe our baby on the go. We got a Pack-and-Play, a porta-swing, a travel high chair... all of which folded down from gargantuan to just plain huge. *Did we really have to bring all of this crap with us wherever we went?*

The answer, we discovered, was a resounding yes. Because here's the plain truth of it: You can *take* your baby somewhere else; babies are both lightweight and compact. BUT you'll still have to bring every last thing you normally use at home. Even if it is just for the afternoon. Seems crazy, but it is 100% true. You can try to do it another way, but in my experience, you'll end up with a miserable baby, a splitting headache, and a grudge against your spouse who convinced you "we don't need that thing for a few hours." Yes we do, and bring me two Advil. Feel free to travel with your portable progeny, but make no mistake: there is no vacationing with a baby. You get a break from exactly nothing. You're just doing your exact same routine while now paying for lodging so you can enjoy a different view out the window during naptime. The reason I bring this up is because I have a clear memory of Mike losing his mind every time we packed the car to visit family or take a trip. Every time. If he were a cartoon, there would have been a speech bubble over his head that read $#@%^&! while steam came bellowing out of his ears. I remember Mike's brother Jeff (having three kids of his own) saying something so simple and wise: *Mike just has to adjust his expectations.* It was a nice way to say, "Get over it. This is what it is." Mike could have saved himself the grief rather than being supremely irritated before every single excursion, thinking this time it would somehow be easier. Sorry, pal. This is what it is... and also why minivans exist.

Essential Sidebar

I don't want to paint a picture of Mike as an irrational person or short-sighted dad. He is neither of these things. Mike's best friend, Will, used the word "reasonable" to describe Mike *three separate times* in his best man toast at our wedding, and there was nodding in the crowd each time. Aside from being oddly triggered by baby gear, Mike is very easygoing and positive. Ask literally anyone who knows him. And just as my dad was a "find the good" role model for me, Mike is definitely that for our kids. Years ago, he added something to our kids' bedtime routine that I am happy to say has stuck. We've come to call it "three things," as in the question, "What are your three things?" Before saying goodnight, we tell each other three things that were good about our day. Pretty quick and fairly simple, but "three things" has served as powerful practice in taking another look to find the good. For all of us. Here are some answers I've recently heard from Michael and Natalie: *We had Chipotle for dinner, my math test wasn't that bad, I had fun at soccer practice, it was sunny today, my square[21] is going to be in the Hoedown in PE, Dad remembered to buy bagels, I took Ruby for a walk.* Even if Mike or I forget to ask, the kids now ask us. They don't seem to want to say goodnight until we've had that little exchange, and I have to say, neither do I. We've all become accustomed to ending the day with this small ritual of optimism and gratitude.

Beware of Extremes

As with anything, you can go too far with this idea. I am not suggesting you adopt a sunshine soldier mentality or deny that a negative event has occurred. Toxic positivity is exactly that. Toxic. As I talked about earlier in the book, we shouldn't pretend that every oyster has a pearl. There's just no reality in that. That said, you probably know someone who fits this description. Someone who fabricates a sacchariney sweet upside to every bummer of a situation. Exhausting, I know. I'm pretty sure these are the same people who decided that it is actually *good luck* to have rain on your wedding day or to encounter a traffic jam when you're already late. Okay, that was Alanis Morrisette. But you get the idea.

On the other hand, there are those folks who choose to see none of the good, even when it is staring them square in the face. Remember Rachel Dratch's *Saturday Night Live* character, Debbie Downer? If not, YouTube can refresh your memory. Debbie was the living embodiment of seeing the negative; she took every opportunity to interject an

---

21   Can you believe the American public school system is still hanging in there with the square dancing? Our high school has a NASA program for crying out loud, but the very same kids are still being asked to do-si-do their partner.

unexpected and tragic factoid into an otherwise upbeat conversation. I was surprised to discover that *Debbie Downer* is actually a term that has been added to the dictionary: *a negative or pessimistic person; a person who speaks only of the bad or depressing aspects of something and lessens the enthusiasm or pleasure of others.* Debbie Downer and her perpetually sunny archnemesis (who I've named Ursula Upside) have each gone too far. They are back to the "always" and "never" rock brain thinking of early childhood. Do you believe Ursula when she says she's had the *most amazing* time at your dinner party and that your pasta fagioli is the best meal she's *ever had?* Probably not, because to her (and Emmett from *The Lego Movie*), everything is awesome. And forget it, after an hour with Debbie, even a nun will be looking for the nearest bar.

Far from the extremes exists a comfy and healthy middle. Where valid and meaningful upsides are often hiding in plain sight, just waiting to be found. That is my entire point here: seek and ye shall find. And when you find these rational upsides, read the room. You don't have to share *every* silver lining with *every* person in your staff meeting, train car, or check-out line. To this, I'll add that it isn't always the easiest thing to find a better view of something because, frankly, we are living in tricky times. In the last few years, we've lived through a global pandemic and its accompanying lockdown—both which came with a significant amount of loss. We've watched universal regard for truth hit an astonishing low, causing our nation to become divided and polarized over a great number of issues. And, as a personal standout for me, we never get a break from grieving for the victims of mass shootings, many of whom are children in school.[22] So, I realize "find the good" can be a big ask. That is not lost on me. Sometimes we really have to flip a scenario on its head to come across something redeeming. But it is a skill we can build, a muscle we can strengthen. And the more I improve, the more I'm convinced that "good" wants to be found.

---

22 According to the *New York Times* and the Gun Violence Archive, over 44,000 people were killed in 648 mass shootings in the United States in 2022.

Continue to Look for Role Models

Well past my formative years, I continued to accumulate role models as I practiced reasonable, glass-half-full thinking. I wasn't actively looking for these people, but I couldn't help but be captivated by them. Two of these people are Bob Ross and Fred Rogers. Along with Michelle Obama, Lin-Manuel Miranda, Conan O'Brien, and Betty White, these two gentle souls would definitely be invited to my ideal-but-pretend dinner party. If you're not familiar, Bob Ross had a long running show on PBS called *The Joy of Painting*. It was actually an instructional show; you could buy the paints and a canvas and join Bob in painting "happy little trees" from your own home. I'm not sure many people did that, but I know millions were enchanted with this big-haired, soft-spoken optimist. To him, there were no mistakes—only "happy accidents." Bob decided that, when it came to art, there was only beauty to be seen. Rather than call an errant brushstroke *a mistake*, he'd invent a backstory as to why this tree was crooked or that roofline was askew. As skilled as he was, he was gentle with himself. And in his trademark soothing voice, he encouraged us to be the same. Just like *The Joy of Painting*, everything about *Mister Rogers' Neighborhood* (also on PBS) was calm and soothing. Over the course of thirty-one years and 900+ episodes, Mister Rogers also spoke directly to his television audience: the children of America. As one

My Bob Ross, Pink Pearl, and Mister Rogers next to my desk at school.

of those children, I can remember feeling like he was talking to no one else but me. Like no one before and no one since, Mister Rogers went into the world of children. Pretend play, simple demonstrations, and conversations with people in the neighborhood were his tools. With these, he addressed children's curiosities, clarified their misconceptions, and quelled their fears. In my opinion, he was the epitome of a child-centered presence. This is why I think of him as my spirit animal: he was what I needed as a child and what I strive to be as an adult. He was the gold standard of acceptance, reassurance, and celebration of childhood.

Our Mini Mentors

When searching for people to look up to, don't forget to look down. I have worked with children my entire career, and I do not mince words when I say kids are smart. Not only that, they are pure and intuitive, can spot insincerity a mile away, and have insight that, frankly, we adults lost a *long* time ago. Children have taught me a myriad of things, from obscure dinosaur facts to profound life lessons. I think this is, in part, because kids don't overthink it. They just experience and react, observe and respond. Unlike adults, they don't overcomplicate things—most kids don't have the attention span for that. Here are some of my favorite bits of "kid wisdom" from the book *Really Important Stuff My Kids Have Taught Me,* by Cynthia Copeland. I highly recommend this book. I keep it on an end table in my family room and flip through it when my perspective needs a realignment.

- If it is in your way, climb over it.
- Ask why until you understand.
- Just keep banging until someone opens the door.
- Crawling still gets you there.
- If you want a kitten, start out asking for a horse.
- If you kick the ball to another kid, he'll probably kick it back.
- Don't worry about crossing the street until you get to the curb.

When my tendency to overthink rears its ugly head, I try to simplify the situation by putting myself in little kid shoes. How would a seven year old see this? What would be their "undercomplicated" conclusion? And many times, this exercise helps me land on a reasonable point of view.

In addition to seeing something as a child, I also adjust my perspective by thinking of how I'd explain something *to* a child. When I am struggling with a worrisome topic, my mind automatically conjures a child-friendly explanation. Maybe it is the teacher in me, or perhaps the mom, but I can't seem to turn it off. I make an attempt to explain, even if it is just to myself in my mind, a difficult concept in a gentle and simple manner. And in finding the words to help imaginary children understand a situation, I see it more clearly myself. I remember using this strategy in May of 2020 when Breonna Taylor and George Floyd were killed just twelve days apart. Here's how that went (including a little bit of context).

Although I have the utmost respect for journalists and the essential work that they do, the news began to feel like one tragic or maddening story after another. Maybe it always had been this way, but after the events in Charlottesville, Virginia, in 2017 and the subsequent coverage, I hit my limit. "Oh FORGET it, I'm OUT!" (*wait...* I think I have said this before...) For my own peace and emotional stability, I decided I needed to stop watching the news on television. Give me weather forecasts, give me sports updates, but I could no longer consume a steady diet of stories featuring the worst of humanity. It was just too much. Keeping self-preservation in mind, I needed to figure out a way to stay informed without the spike of anger and despair that came with watching the nightly news. So I came up with a two-pronged hack that I've used on and off (but mostly on) since 2017: I get the *gist* of the headlines from late night talk show monologues followed by the first two minutes of the Today Show. I know, I know, that first prong is not exactly hard-hitting journalism, but I'll take a little bias for the comedy that makes these stories tolerable. Most mornings I watch one or two monologues from the night before as I drink my coffee and unload the dishwasher. Then I "check in" with Savannah and Hoda as they run down the headlines that broke overnight. If I see a story I'm interested in and want to know more, I find a news article from a trustworthy source.

But after Breonna Taylor and George Floyd were killed on May 13th and 25th, 2020, I could not look away. Their stories hit me hard. Like many Americans, I had anger that I had no idea where to put or how to process. Typically, my go-to negative emotions are sadness, worry, guilt, fear... but not anger. Rarely anger. But in May of 2020, I had a lot of it. And my outrage was two-fold. One: the killing of Black Americans at the hands of law enforcement was occurring at an alarmingly, terrifying rate. And two: many people still didn't see the problem. Each time I heard "all lives matter" as a rebuttal meant to cut down the legitimacy of the Black Lives Matter movement, I wanted to scream. I won't say any more on the social politics of this matter because I don't want to alienate you any further if we're not on the same metaphorical page here; that is not my intent and not why you are reading this book. It's just the backdrop of the narrative I'm about to share. The following is what I wrote to help me process the harrowing events of May 2020. Because it was just for me, I didn't share this with anyone at the time, but I do want to offer it to you as an example of choosing your perspective.

Talking with a group of children, I told them that our friends, the Hawksbill sea turtles, were in trouble. If people did not help, the sea turtles would continue to get hurt and die. Understandably, the children had many questions. Where do the Hawksbills live? How big are they? What do they eat? Why do people want to hurt them? *Some of these questions have simple answers. Hawksbill sea turtles live in coral reefs with millions of other living things. They weigh anywhere between ninety and one hundred fifty pounds, and they are about thirty-five inches long. Hawksbills eat sponges from the reef's surface. This actually helps other fish get to their food, which helps the health of the entire reef ecosystem. Their last question I couldn't answer as easily.*

Naturally, the children wanted to help. What can we do? *Well, I told them, we just need to use our voices to let people know what we know. The Hawksbill Sea turtles need our help. They are important to coral reefs. They are beautiful, they are God's creatures, and they deserve protection. They matter.*

Most of the children were on board immediately. They took out paper and crayons and set about to tackle the mission before them. A few, though, remained pensive. But aren't other animals important, too? Don't we need to help the rhinos and the tigers and the pets that need to be rescued? *These children are asking with love in their hearts. And they are right; many animals need protecting. And all of them need care and respect.*

I collect my thoughts and gently explain that, of course, all life is precious. I agree. But for today, this effort is going to focus on the Hawksbills because they are very threatened right now. I explain to my concerned friends that sea turtles are in danger because they are losing their nesting and feeding habitats. There is a long list of other threats: excessive egg collection, pollution, wildlife trade, and coastal development.

For many, many years, these turtles have faced so much hardship. I pause to let this sink in. After a moment of quiet, I say, I love that you care about all animals. I care about all animals, too. But right now, there is a sea turtle emergency. It is okay that our effort, this effort, is just about sea turtles.

This doesn't mean there isn't love in your hearts for other animals. At this moment, though, the Hawksbills need us most. It's important that they have their own movement. After everything that has happened, they should have their own movement. This seemed to reassure my friends. They nodded in understanding. And with peace in their hearts and crayons in their hands, they joined the others.[23]

---

23 Two things: One—I know that the harrowing events of May 2020 represent hundreds of Georges and hundreds of Breonnas. I mourn for them all. Two—I realize the insensitivity of comparing Black people to animals. I don't condone that direct comparison. But children love animals. Many see themselves as animal protectors. The metaphor was just a vehicle to tap into their compassion using something familiar. So, I am asking for your understanding on this. The Hawksbill Sea turtles are real, and the challenges they face are also real. However, the story and the children in it are fictional.

Set Your Default to *Benefit of the Doubt*

Seeing something in a more understanding or gentle light is a choice we can make. I consider it to be low hanging fruit on a tree of happiness. It costs nothing to give someone or something the benefit of the doubt. Kara did that for me during our first week of college; she chose to see the good person underneath the tear-stained high school dance team t-shirt. She assumed that I was the better of two options. In these situations, your perspectives are always written in pencil. If more information comes to light that prompts you to change your mind, well, then get out your Pink Pearl and change it. It's your superpower, remember?

The following is a benefit-of-the-doubt reflection I wrote in December of 2021. The inspiration for it, again, goes back to children—this time my own. I wanted to take a different perspective on something I'd always considered to be a little problematic (albeit accepted). With Michael and Natalie in mind, I found the *better of two options* vantage point that addressed the troubling nature of something that, I believe, had always been well-intended.

The Unasked Question

I began preparing for it when my children were very young. In my mind, I started working on the answer to what I thought *would be an inevitable question. I was sure that someday Michael and Natalie would want to know if Santa Claus was "real." I was determined to give them a more satisfying answer than just yes or no. Much to my surprise, neither of them asked. However, there were hints along the way that gave us a window into their ever-evolving thinking on the subject of magical visitors.*

- *Mom, Santa is a person. But the Easter Bunny is a* bunny. *Is the real Easter Bunny just a person in a bunny costume? Where does he* even live?
- *Dylan and Bridget don't have a chimney. If Santa can get into their house without one, why can't he just go in everyone's house that way? And what* even IS *that way?*

- *There is just no way reindeer can fly. They weigh, like, a thousand pounds. Bats are the only mammals that can fly.*
- *Mom, why did the Easter Bunny give me jelly beans?* (Chin goes down and to the side, eyebrows go up) *Doesn't he know that I don't like jelly beans...?*
- *Mom, the tooth fairy took my tooth even though I left a note under my pillow saying I wanted to keep it. Can she give it back to me tonight?* (Same chin/eyebrow routine, different kid).

In these moments, Mike and I would exchange panicked glances, trip over half-baked answers, or simply join them in their complete and justified confusion. I can only assume that parents everywhere can relate.

There comes a point, however, when we want *our children to think through situations that seem beyond the bounds of possibility or contradict things they know for sure. Would we want our eventual teenagers still believing that one man could visit every country in the world in one night? Of course not. We educate our kids to be problem solvers, to connect learned information, and to question things that don't add up. This is age-appropriate growth. But what, then, becomes of the magic of Christmas?*

Knowing that the question "Is Santa Claus real?" did not have a simple answer, I made it my mission to craft an explanation that was both historical and inspirational. I'd had a general awareness that there was an actual person, at some point in history, named St. Nicholas. However, I didn't have any idea how he got so many aliases or how elves and flying reindeer became a part of his narrative.

No surprise, the internet provided me with a lengthy history filled with contradictory accounts of this real man's life. Among the less debated details are the fact that he lived during the 3rd century, was born in present-day Turkey, loved children, and lived a life in service to God. Beyond this, my deep-dive led me to a number of legends which may or may not have a foothold in truth. As I read through the lore, I found myself hoping to find something magical. But true to form, the rabbit hole that is the internet left me feeling drained and forgetful of the point of my quest.

After some time away, I reminded myself of my original purpose: I wasn't writing a term paper on the man; I just wanted to have something meaningful to say to my kids when they asked how they "really" got all of those gifts. To that end, I took the liberty of combining the most inspiring parts of the stories I found and molding them into a magical truth that, I believed, would work for my family.

Because they never asked, this explanation sat on the shelf in my mind for more than a few Christmases. Though seemingly content with their own conclusions about Christmas magic, I still wanted to share with them, at ages fourteen and twelve, the answer to an unasked question that took my mind and heart over a decade to synthesize. So here it is. This is what I have now shared with Michael and Natalie. Perhaps you'll find something here worthy of sharing, too.

Santa Claus was a real person. He really lived. But as people do, he grew old and he passed away. His real name was Nicholas, but it seems that he did not have a wife. Nicholas did not live in a cold part of the world, but because of his connection to Christmas, we think of him as living in a cold, snowy place. The name Santa Claus came from Nicholas's Dutch nickname, Sinter Klaas, a shortened form of Sint Nikolaas.

Although he did not have children of his own, Nicholas always loved children. It is said that each Christmas, he gave handmade presents to all of the children in his village. He did this for many years. When he passed away, the village parents took up the charge and continued to give gifts to their children on his behalf; these gifts were "from" Nicholas. Because he had started something selfless and beautiful, they carried on his tradition and, ultimately, helped create his legacy.

The gifts you get from Santa each Christmas are a continuation of this legacy. Along with families all over the world, we honor this great man by keeping his annual tradition alive.

The real Nicholas, who was sainted for his kindness, valued two things that we value: generosity and community. He was generous with *his time, his talent, and his resources. He didn't travel the world to give gifts to every child; he took care of the people around him. One person cannot give so much to so many. But all of us can be generous with what we do have and love the people who are right around us. Your gifts on Christmas morning come to you because a real man and his real community inspired the world to do just that. And that is nothing short of magical.*

When I was in elementary school, I read many books from the *Choose Your Own Adventure* series. Have you come across these? They are structured so that the reader makes decisions as the main character, therefore influencing the story's path and outcome. For example, Chapter One might start like this: *You are walking to school one day when you notice something peculiar...* You read a few pages and are presented with a choice: *To board the hot air balloon, turn to page 9. To continue to search for the dog on foot, turn to page II.* You could read the book thirty-plus times and take a unique path each time. And you could revise your choices by going back a step. I got to thinking what a good metaphor this is; as the main characters in our own lives, we take a perspective and travel down a corresponding path. *If you choose to ghost the friend that has been ignoring you the last few months because enough is enough already, turn to page 8. If you are concerned and want to find out what is going on in her life that may have caused this extended period of disconnection, turn to page II.* What made those books fun was the chance to steer the ship. In life, we really have that ability. Just as *both are true, and that works, too*—there are many options here. An abundance of written-in-pencil perspectives that you can try on for size. All you have to do is listen to your heart, make a choice, and turn the corresponding page.

Takeaway Five

NO DAY BUT TODAY

> *"There's only us; there's only this. Forget regret, or life is yours to miss..."* —Jonathan Larson

B oth the title of this chapter and its beginning quote come from *Another Day*, a song from the Broadway musical, *Rent*. Maybe you've seen the movie if you haven't had the chance to see it live on stage (which I highly recommend). Two central themes of this poignant masterpiece are that *time is fleeting* and *life is fragile*. These are things we all know to be true, but until something tragic happens, we tend to forget. I think you would agree that this is merciful; no one needs to be walking through their day-to-day life continually lamenting their eventual demise. We've got enough on our plates just trying to recall the password we just created but didn't write down, because "I'll remember that." No, you won't. Tragic things are *going* to happen, and when they do, we get a cold, sharp reminder that time waits for no man and tomorrow is promised to no one. Sorry to bring you down. Reflecting can be a bummer sometimes. But, thankfully, we have tools to help take us back up: perspectives that can be revised, apologies that can be sincerely offered, and lifers on whom we can lean. Not to mention the knowledge that Plans B through Z are valid and filled with potential. And of course, our *now-sung* hero still in our pockets—the mighty Pink Pearl.

Sometimes it takes enduring or witnessing a tragedy to refocus on the trajectory of our own lives. I can remember many times in which I've felt guilt over learning (i.e. benefitting) from someone else's hardship. That felt selfish and, on some level, even cruel. How could I gain from someone else's distress? But in taking a different perspective on it, I realized I wouldn't mind someone learning from my bumpy road. It wouldn't change the bump's impact on me, and it would be a way to extract more good from a bad situation. In fact, you learning from my bumpy road is why I am writing this book to begin with... and perhaps why you have decided to read it. Learning from each other is a gift we get to both give and receive. Goodbye guilt; hello gratitude.

So, when it has been my turn to experience a painful turn-of-events, this is what I have learned. First, face it, and let yourself feel it. If it hurts, be hurt. If it causes anger, be angry. If you try to avoid it, you're going to give your inner-Ursula an ulcer. Then catch your breath, and get your bearings. When you are ready, figure out a new place to stand, look again, and find a takeaway. Remember, we don't *have* to do this; we *get* to do this. Ask yourself: What is life teaching me here? What does the universe want me to notice? This is *getting back up* after life pushes us down. It is the consolation prize that comes with being reminded that all of our earthly lives are written in pencil.

When life shows you how fragile it is, take the opportunity to review where you are and where you want to go. Look at the big picture. Are there priorities you are ignoring? What do you want to say to people? What do you want to accomplish? You get this one life; what do you want most from it? The answers are in there; put down your electronic device long enough for them to come to you. And if some of them seem a little too ambitious or challenging, that is okay. Confidence is not a prerequisite for doing a difficult thing; it is the *result* of doing a difficult thing.

After some me-time reflection (I enjoy going outdoors for this), grab your pencil and make two lists. Right here in this book if you want. The first is what I call the *over-the-top* list—all the things you would want to do if money wasn't a consideration and/or success was guaranteed. Take a year off to hike the Appalachian Trail? Learn to fly a plane? Run for a seat in the US Senate? At the moment, my over-the-top list has one thing on it. I would love to go on an exhaustive European tour with my kids, spending most of our time in Italy. While there, I would want to go to Formia, my Centola family hometown. I'd love to see if we have any relatives still living there, and if so, make arrangements to meet. Are there things I could do now to help at least *some of* that dream become a reality? Sure, and those things can be added to the second list, called the *totally-doable-with-the-resources-available* list. No years of saving or special skills required. Do you want to reconnect with someone with whom you lost touch? Convert all of your grandparents' old photographs to a digital format? Learn to play guitar? For me, I could learn Italian on an app like Duolingo or start a separate bank account for travel savings. Unrelated to European travel, I would love to take my kayak out more often, and maybe find others in my area who want to do the same. You're holding in your hands my latest "second list" project, and I bet you have an idea for one, too. But no pressure—nothing is etched in stone here. You're just brainstorming in pencil, so unlike every password we swore we'd remember, write it down. You'll be glad you have something to reference.

For me, the idea of *No Day but Today* is where it all comes together. If you turn back to the Table of Contents, all the chapters before this one connect right here. In almost any order, these topics intersect, overlap, and lead us back to the present moment. For example, bumpy roads can lead to finding your people which can lead to seeing things differently which can help you to realize that more than one thing is true, and so on. Because of this, most of my personal anecdotes could fit neatly inside multiple chapters. Mrs. Tenenbaum the art teacher: *Both are True* but also *Choosing Your Perspective*. Michael and the soccer B team: *Bumpy Road* but also *Finding Your People*. There is nothing linear or absolute about what we experience. Life doesn't promise that, so like Mike and baby gear, we just have to adjust our expectations. We have to look at what we can choose and what we can change, including our perspective from behind the wheel, the people with whom we travel, and the routes and detours we want to take.

The big exception here, of course, is when someone dies. The finality of this goodbye and the knowledge that you have to live out your days *without them* is about as jarring as it gets. I think it is beyond our human sensibilities to conceive of such a cruel permanence, but we have to accept it nonetheless. Over time, though, a feature of grief and loss has presented itself to me… At first, I thought it was a fluke, but since it has happened a number of times now, I really think there is something to it. When someone I love passes on, I seem to "get" something of theirs that now lives on through me. And typically, it has been something that I had considered to be a big part of who they were. The first time this happened was in 2001 when my Aunt Sally Levedag died suddenly at age fifty-four. She had this unmistakably boisterous, full-of-life laugh, and I loved it. In fact, I stood up at her memorial and shared that, in my deepest moments of sadness, I would think of her laugh, and it would make me smile. And, as if by magic, my own laugh became bigger. Louder. More boisterous. It became just like hers. I joke around that my kids will never lose me because, eventually, I'll laugh, and they'll find me. Recently, my friend Audra told me that even though she didn't see me from across the soccer field, she knew I was at the game because she could hear me laughing. I fully believe this is my Aunt Sally shining her light through me. In this way, I don't have to go on without her. I can go on *with* her.

I wrote the following reflection in November of 2022 in response to losing two beloved people in my life. I didn't think it fit in this book until I realized that pencil markings are also fragile and fleeting. Ask any lefty, and they'll tell you that dragging the heel of your hand across words you just wrote in pencil results in a smudged, blurry haze. If you want to save something for years and years, you wouldn't choose to write it in pencil. Permanence isn't one of a pencil's features; it is the opposite by design. Our earthly existences are similar—we are not permanent. What we have is the present moment. We have today.

Let me know if you need anything. *We say these words to friends, neighbors, and co-workers when something unfortunate happens. You've probably had people say them to you when you were struggling. And these are sincere offers, I believe. We extend a hand by bringing a meal or sending a card. I don't know about you, but it is a rare event when I reach back out and say, "Yes, actually, there is something you can do…" But I think we should. I think we should take each other up on these genuine offers to "do something." Because, undoubtedly, in these moments, something is needed.*

I've been prompted to reflect on this idea a few times this year. 2022 has been hard on my heart, so lately I have been the recipient of the "need anything" offers. Over the course of eight months, I have lost two men for whom I care deeply. One a friend, one a family member. There was no car accident, they were not taken by cancer or heart disease, they were not "old." They won't get to be old, in fact. And in all honesty, neither of these people would have chosen to leave the auditorium before the final curtain call. I am sure of it, because it would contradict everything about how they lived their very full lives. But something happened. Something that we, as a national community, don't want to talk about. You offered to "do something." Well, here it is. If you are not okay, please don't say that you are. That's the "anything" I'm letting you know I need.

Of course, I'm not suggesting you spill the contents of your troubled soul to the first person to say, "Hey, how are you?" (We'd have to train and compensate Walmart greeters very differently if we did.) But find your person and say, "You know, something just doesn't feel right lately. I can't put my finger on it, though. Do you have some time to let me process it out loud?" Okay, those are my words. Pick your own. Or tell an impartial stranger with a degree in this stuff, either in-person or online. Or, if you don't notice the changes yourself, trust your loved ones when they ask, "Is everything okay? You don't seem like yourself." They know the comfortable, mentally healthy you. So, your spouse, best friend, or child might notice something's up even before you do. Trust that observation. It is important and reliable data.

Now I am not a medical professional, so, admittedly, the following is part logical assumption, part gross oversimplification of the complex inner workings of the human body. When there is too much of something or not enough of another, our bodies can't always compensate. Without enough Vitamin A, people can suffer from night blindness. Too much iron can lead to liver disease. If hormone levels are too high or too low, it could result in an endocrine disorder such as underactive thyroid or Grave's disease. My point is this: our bodies are meant to stay in balance. It is not inconsistent, then, for our brains to require a certain biochemical balance to maintain our well-being. When the biochemical functions of our brain are not what they need to be, our mental health suffers. I believe this includes our decision-making skills, our ability to assess the severity and permanence of different sets of circumstances, and the overall inability to see any path that could return us to a comfortable existence.

So, yes, I do need something. And if I may be so bold, I need it right away. Do not ignore mental health—yours or someone else's. Don't "fake it until you make it." Don't wait for things to magically improve. Take seriously what you feel, and put stock in what your loved ones observe. Say, "No, actually, I don't think I'm okay right now," and accept the support that will undoubtedly follow. It is how you will end up where we need you and where you truly belong: comfortably in your seat when the orchestra finishes the postlude and the house lights come on.

Please know that no matter what you decide to keep or what you decide to erase in this life you've been given, it is important that you are here. The world has been given just one *you*, and you are needed. Your worth does not come from your chosen path. It is not diminished by your mistakes; it is not amplified by your successes. **You have worth because you are the one and only you.** That's all. It cannot change because you will never stop being you. There is a song I like called "Beautiful World" by Jim Brickman and Adam Crossley. It is from the 2009 album of the same name. Truthfully, some of the lyrics don't make sense to me, but there is one line that is repeated, by my count, six times: "It's a beautiful world; we're all here." It is so simple, but it really says it all. You are part of the "we" that makes this world beautiful. You are a part of everything I've written here.

* * *

This is my memory journal. When someone dies, I make an entry for them, including their name, nicknames/what I called them, their birthday and the day they died. Then I list all the little things I can remember about them. Usually, once I get going, I can write page after page. Re-reading my journal allows me to recall the unique, special person they were. These pages are part of my entry about Italia (Tillie) Marucci Panara Pour aka Gram: Mike's grandmother, Natalie's namesake, and one of my favorite people of all time.

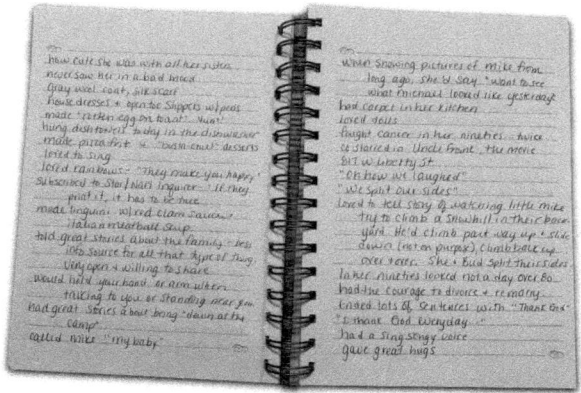

CONCLUSION

> *"There is no joy in possession*
> *without sharing."* —Erasmus

These ideas have taken up space in my head for quite a while, so thank you for letting them vacation in yours. You've been a most gracious host. As a reminder, I have offered up these ideas for both your consideration and critique. Maybe you found something thought-provoking or relatable; I'm hoping so. Maybe you think I am crazy and will now use this book as a prop under that chair with the broken leg. I'm good with that, too. Because you took the time to read and consider these ideas. Plus, it would be super hypocritical of me to say, "YES! This is IT. This the way things ARE" in a book called *Life is Written In Pencil*. I'm sure that there are things written here that I would now choose to erase and/or rewrite. But, if I waited and revised long enough to be sure of every word, this book would never see the light of day.

Please don't think that, just because I've learned (and re-learned) all of these lessons, I follow their teachings all the time. I don't. I can be just as impulsive, irrational, and short-sighted as the next guy. And I've made a ton of mistakes. But I'm working at it, just like you are. And, although this is the book I wish I had when I was graduating from high school, I guess I had to live it to learn it.

If I had to pinpoint the big picture takeaway, it would be this: **there is no arriving, only evolving**. And to evolve, we have to stop long enough to reflect on our experiences. Stop long enough to think about our goals, challenge our assumptions, and feel what our hearts are telling us. That takes some time. Some device-and-media-free time. But the sad truth is we live in a world where we are both overscheduled and drowning in input, so allowing for this time is a challenge. *Stopping* and *reflecting* will need to become things we actively choose to do. We need to carve out time for this, because it is how we figure out what is making us happy or preventing us from living the life we want. And this will need to be an ongoing process, because even if we achieve what we consider to be a totally fulfilling existence, we are still traveling on the bumpy road of life. There will be unexpected detours. There will be mistakes. There will be new interests or circumstances that pull us down an untraveled road. And there will be other people using *their* Pink Pearls, erasing things we'd just as soon keep in place forever. For all of these reasons, course-correcting is here to stay.

Because of this, I chose to include the phrase *finding your best life in plans B through Z* in the title of this book. Initially, I used it to describe my exit from full-time classroom teaching, but moving from one plan to the next isn't limited to career changes. It refers to anytime you thought one thing was "the way things are supposed to be" and then it changed. It reflects shifts in all sorts of things: relationships, perspectives, where you live, groups with whom you affiliate, and so on. Everything that is written in pencil. Some new plans are simple; others are truly life-changing. A few examples come to mind: Mike chose to switch to a vegan diet after his brother suffered and survived a heart-attack at a young age. Also, Mike was forced to find a new job after being laid off when his company, where he would have happily stayed, was bought-out. I chose to raise our children in the Episcopal church (as opposed to where they were baptized) because I wanted an institution where women could hold the highest positions and everyone could marry the person they loved. In each example, Mike and I had been doing one thing but shifted to another. By force or by choice, we tried something new. We picked up our autobiographical pencils, did some editing, and a new plan was born.

Organizational psychologist Dr. Tal Ben-Shahar coined the term *arrival fallacy*: the **false** assumption that once you reach a goal, you will experience enduring happiness. I agree with that idea, maybe because every finish line is also a starting line. Just ask any high school graduate heading out into the world.

But, like all graduates, you made it to the end. And I hope it isn't a leap to say that you actually *thought* about some of the ideas I have proposed. And that's a win for both of us (because this whole time I've felt like we were in this together; didn't you?)

So, to your mind, what did I get right? What do I need to rethink? Open your laptop and get some thoughts recorded. Or better yet, write *right* here the margins, in the blank pages in the back, anywhere and everywhere. Just do yourself a favor. Use a pencil.

Send anything from inklings to book announcements to melissa@beautifulpinkeraser.com.

You already have a fan.

APPENDIX

> *"The beauty of quotes is that they
> all us to glimpse into another's mind
> and understand how they think and
> look at the world."* —Joseph Geran III

A quote about quotes? Okay, now she's gone too far.

The following is probably not the true purpose of an appendix, but if a book is anything like a human body, we don't really need one anyway. But, hey, this may be the only book I ever write, so I'm giving *this* book's appendix a job of my choosing. And the chance to possibly be your favorite part of this book.

I think it is safe to say that you've gotten to know me over the last bunch of chapters, so I am sure this will come as no surprise: I love collecting quotes, lyrics, precepts, aphorisms, and

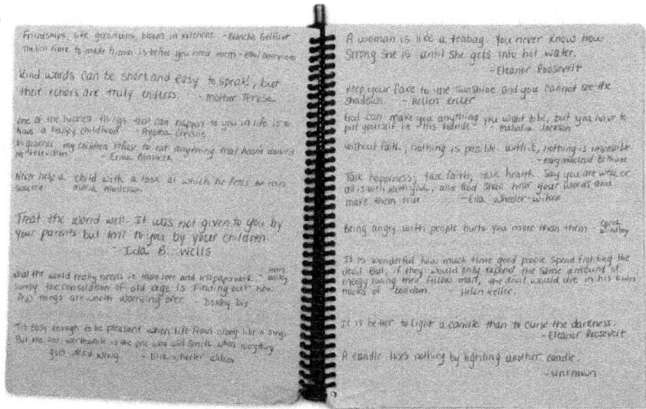

A few pages from my own quote journal.

adages. Eloquent little bits of wisdom that provide a boost or an insight. I've kept a little spiral bound journal filled with them since I was a teenager. To paraphrase Buddy the Elf, I just like words; words are my favorite. My friend Angela used to belong to a quote *club*—like a book club but for people who didn't have the time or inclination to read an entire book.[24] Brilliant. Sign me up.

Here are a few favorite quotes that didn't quite fit somewhere else or would have made some other part of this book too cumbersome. I'll let you decide where they would have fit best. And, as with everything I've offered here, sift through for what rings true. (I also love a good rhyme, but that one was completely serendipitous.)

- "What day is it? asked Pooh. It's today, squeaked Piglet. My favorite day, said Pooh." —A. A. Milne
- "Never help a child with a task at which he feels he can succeed." —Maria Montessori
- "We make a living by what we get. We make a life by what we give." —Winston Churchill
- "It is difficult to make a man miserable while he feels worthy of himself and claims kindred to the great God who made him." —Abraham Lincoln
- "Be who you are and say what you feel... because those who mind don't matter, and those who matter don't mind." —Dr. Seuss
- "In the middle of every difficulty is opportunity." —Albert Einstein
- "Time is a peculiar thing—when you're sad, there's too much of it, and when you're happy, there's never enough." —Billy Crystal, quoting his grandfather
- "The deeper that sorrow carves into your being, the more joy it can contain." —Kahlil Gibran, The Prophet
- "We cannot direct the wind, but we can adjust the sails." —Bertha Calloway
- "To get the full value of a joy, you must have somebody to divide it with." —Mark Twain

---

24 I do love reading whole books, just to clarify.

- "The cure for anything is salt water... sweat, tears, or the sea." —Isak Dinesin
- "People can think you are a horse or a vacuum cleaner. It doesn't *make you* a horse or a vacuum cleaner." —Unknown
- "Prayer is you talking to God. Intuition is God talking to you." —Dr. Wayne Dyer
- "We don't see things as they are... we see them as *we* are." —Anais Nin
- "Changing your mind doesn't make you a flip-flopper or a hypocrite. It means you were open to learning." —Adam Grant
- "When you talk, you are only repeating what you already know. But if you listen, you may learn something new." —Dalai Lama
- "Isn't it fantastic that you can change your mind and create all these happy things?" —Bob Ross
- "When we share our stories, we are reminded of the humanity in each other. And when we take the time to understand each other's stories, we become more forgiving, more empathetic, and more inclusive." —Michelle Obama
- "You don't have to be anything more than who you are right now... There's no person in the whole world like you." —Fred Rogers[25]
- "You are perfectly cast in your life. I can't imagine anyone but you in the role. Go play." —Lin-Manuel Miranda

If words are my favorite, then words combined with music are my favorite times infinity.[26] Even though I have *almost zero* God-given musical talent, music has always been very important to me. It transports me to other times of my life, and it helps me feel connected to those learning similar lessons, finding similar takeaways, navigating similar hardships, or just celebrating the joy of being alive. I love so many kinds of music from so many eras—one more thing I can

---

25   Read as many Mister Rogers quotes as you can. I wanted to include them all, but books of them already exist... and for good reason. Fred Rogers was simple in his wisdom, steadfast in his support of young children, and the very embodiment of human acceptance. I aspire to be all of these things.
26   I spend a lot of time with little kids. Thank you for your understanding.

attribute to my dad's influence. My family, friends, and co-workers will attest to the fact that I have music playing for the majority of my waking hours, and it is also likely that I am singing and/or dancing along.[27] In college, I had to make a cassette tape of songs without lyrics called "The Study Mix" because I found that I was trying to read my textbooks *and sing along to the radio* at the same time. When I first discovered Napster—one of the original web-based music sharing sites—I spent so much time downloading "free" music that it is a wonder I didn't fail out of grad school. If you are so inclined, take a listen to a few favorites in two of my big-feels categories:

1. Upbeat and Joyful:
   - "A Great Day to Be Alive," Travis Tritt
   - "Odds Are," Barenaked Ladies
   - "All About Soul," Billy Joel
   - "Catch My Disease," Ben Lee
   - "King of Anything," Sara Bareilles
   - "Daydream Believer," The Monkees
   - "Bruises," Train featuring Ashley Monroe
   - "Closer to Fine," Indigo Girls
   - "AM Gold," Train
   - "River Bank," Brad Paisley
   - "I'm Still Standing," Elton John
   - "Uptight (Everything's Alright)," Stevie Wonder

2. Sentimental and Contemplative:
   - "For Good," Original Broadway cast of *Wicked*
   - "Seasons of Love," Original Broadway cast of *Rent*
   - "For Baby," John Denver
   - "Things We've Handed Down," Marc Cohn
   - "Oooh Child," The Five Stairsteps

---

27   My sister finds endless entertainment in catching me singing when I don't think anyone is listening. Sometimes I DO know, but I throw her a bone and belt it out anyway.

- "Rainbow," Kacey Musgraves
- "In My Life," The Beatles
- "Slow Down," Ben Jelen
- "Let Them Be Little," Billy Dean
- "Against the Wind," Bob Seger
- "Stones in the Road," Mary Chapin Carpenter

I am humbled to include the obituary of Alice Tenenbaum, my seventh-grade art teacher who passed away in 2018, almost thirty years after I'd left her classroom. She remains my strongest and most poignant proof that none of us are just one thing.

Alice Tenenbaum was born on April 22, 1930 in what was then Czechoslovakia. Her large, close-knit family enjoyed wealth and privilege, but that was torn away from her at age fourteen, when she and her family were shipped to Auschwitz. Of the twenty close family members who went with her to the concentration camp, only she and her mother survived Auschwitz and the death march to Bergen Belsen.

After World War II, Alice lived briefly in Sweden and then she and her mother traveled to America penniless to start life anew. At age twenty, she married Sol Tenenbaum and they remained happily married until his death in 1997.

Although Alice never finished middle school, she managed to convince Hofstra University to admit her. While raising her family, Alice earned both Bachelor's and Master's degrees from Hofstra University. She then taught art at Northport High School on Long Island for more than twenty years. She was also an accomplished artist and sculptor.

Alice was fluent in eight languages and enjoyed fashion and design. She traveled the world, visiting six continents, and enjoyed playing tennis and skiing. She was also the reigning ping-pong champion among her friends and family.

After Sol's death, Alice met Hy Flugman who was her constant companion for almost twenty years, until his death in 2017. During her active retirement, Alice was a docent at the Museum of Jewish Heritage and gave lectures about the Holocaust at conferences and for school groups. She was the inspiration for a book and was featured in two documentaries. She was also an avid and accomplished bridge player.

Alice loved New York City and all it had to offer and loved spending time with her family. Her persistence and strength served as an inspiration for her family and her zest for life will be truly missed. May she be remembered for all the lives she touched, including her friends, students, many admirers, and especially her family.

To lighten things up, here are some college memories that will only be hilarious to some.

Here is our version of this real book. I've included two pages of the six I wrote. Redactions included to protect the innocent and/or short-sighted. We were just kids, after all.

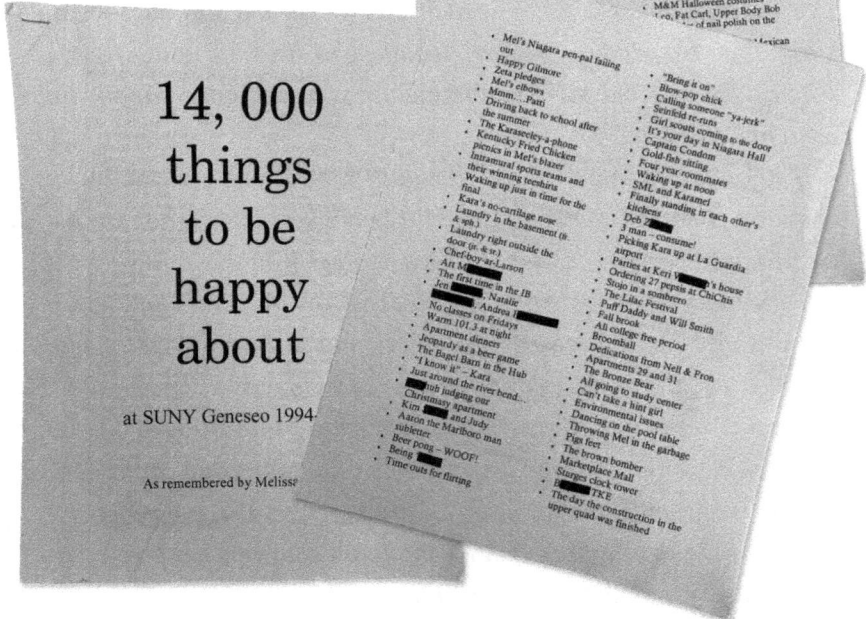

14, 000
things
to be
happy
about

at SUNY Geneseo 1994

As remembered by Melissa

- 0.0 boy
- Syncronizing our stereos
- Learning through osmosis
- Pa Stojo
- Turbo cups
- Tyler comes back from England
- Quotes from Random RJ patrons
- Megan
- Writing on IB walls
- Friday night wings
- Sharing gallons of milk
- Hamburger helper
- Barenaked Ladies
- Geneseo Knightline
- parties at ZBXi

- Parents in the IB
- Tuff mutt
- Toner, Audra, Miceli's Deli
- Never joining sororities
- Getting your first college A
- Dr. Bob's phone call
- 's "shut uppa"
- Growing up together
- Kara a.k.a. Rasheem
- Losing our keys
- Haunted hayrides?

- Quarter drafts
- Norbert Lahay
- Ames circulars
- Being invited out for Valentine's Day — by John
- Tara Dertao comes to Geneseo
- M&M Halloween costumes
- co, Fat Carl, Upper Body Bob
- of nail polish on the
- exican

- Mel's Niagara pen-pal failing out
- Happy Gilmore
- Zeta pledges
- Mel's elbows
- Mmm... Patti
- Driving back to school after the summer
- The Karaseeley-a-phone
- Kentucky Fried Chicken picnics in Mel's blazer
- Intramural sports teams and their winning t-shirts
- Waking up just in time for the final
- Kara's no-cartilage now
- Laundry in the basement (6 & sph.)
- Laundry right outside the door (p. & yr.)
- Chef-boy-ar-Larson
- Art M
- The first time in the IB
- Natalie
- No classes on Fridays — Andrea
- Warm 101.3 at night
- Apartment dinners
- Jeopardy as a beer game
- The Bagel Barn in the Hub
- "I know it" - Kara
- Just around the river bend
- Christmas apartment
- Kim and Judy
- Aaron the Marlboro man
- Beer pong – WOOF!
- Being
- Time outs for flirting

- "Bring it on"
- Blow-pop chick
- Calling someone "ya-jerk"
- Seinfeld re-runs
- Girl scouts coming to the door
- It's your day in Niagara Hall
- Captain Condom
- Gold-fish sitting
- Four year roommates
- Waking up at noon
- SML and Karamel
- Finally standing in each other's kitchen
- Deb Z
- 3 man – consume!
- Picking Kara up at La Guardia airport
- Parties at Keri V's house
- Ordering 27 pepsis at ChiChis
- Stoli in a sombrero
- The Lilac Festival
- Puff Daddy and Will Smith
- Fall brook
- All college free period
- Broomball
- Dedications from Nell & Fron
- Apartments 29 and 31
- The Bronze Bear
- All going to study center
- Can't take a hint girl
- Environmental issues
- Dancing on the pool table
- Throwing Mel in the garbage
- Pigs feet
- The brown bomber
- Marketplace Mall
- Sturges clock tower
- TKE
- The day the construction in the upper quad was finished

And, as promised, my Aunt Mary Centola's sauce recipe. I am going to have to insist that when you serve it, you tell everyone at the table that they are too skinny and have to eat, eat.

NT MARYS TOMATO SAUCE WITH SAUSAGE & MEATBALLS

INGREDIENTS FOR 2 PEOPLE
2 Large cans Delmonte Tomato Sauce + 3/4 can of water
4 links of sweet italian sausage
2 links of hot italian sausage (cut these in half)
- Garlic Powder - 2 tablespoons
Parsley Flakes - 2 tablespoons
Basil Flakes - 2 tablespoons
Black Pepper - no salt in cooking this sauce
Italian Olive Oil - 3 tablespoons

MEATBALLS - FOR 2 PEOPLE   Garlic Powder - 1 tbsp
1/2 lb. chop meat   1 Egg
1/2 cup italian grated cheese   Seasoned Bread Crumbs (1/4 cup)
Parsley Flakes - 2 tbsp. ———   6 oz cold water + Mix
                                       if too dry add more water

Directions for Aunt Mary's Tomato Sauce with Meat [Page 2 of 2]
In large pot, add olive oil & sausage; when sausage is brown, add tomato Sauce + water, also all dry ingredients - do not add salt to this. While that is cooking on low flame, start to mix your chop meat with all the ingredients listed. When you add the cold water to this, if it feels to dry, gradually add more water. Mix well, then form your meatballs for frying. When done, put the meatballs into the same pot of Tomato Sauce along with the Sausage & cook for 3 hours. Enjoy!!

note - You can double/or triple the amount for more people and freeze any left over.

ACKNOWLEDGMENTS

> *"But people need lift, too. People don't get moving, they don't soar, they don't achieve great heights, without something [or someone] buoying them up."* —Elizabeth Wein

As it turns out, I took my own advice—the advice I was offering five specific high school graduates (Meg, Luke, Stephen, Tristan and Maggie) in my little homemade card. *Try something interesting, and see where it takes you.* Thanks to the encouragement of my cousin and friend Cindy Urbanski, I tried writing a book, and I love where it has taken me.

Cindy—Thank you for saying, "Your words are important and need to be out in the world." That opinion resulted in my having both bravery and momentum. And, even though you were 725 miles away, you held my hand the entire time I bumped along this new and sometimes intimidating road. You gave me the counsel and reassurance I needed to turn a little poem into an entire book, one that would not exist without your support and enthusiasm. You are a gifted writer and coach, a treasured friend, and just a fantastic human. I love you and truly cannot thank you enough.

To the talented women at Synergy Publishing Group. The word "synergy" could not be a more fitting descriptor. Thank you for lending your expertise, your artistry, and your guidance to my project. I am beyond grateful.

To my friends Hennessey Lustica, Christine Scoppa, Michelle Corey, Melanie Mroz, and Jenny Giessler. You listened to my stories and convinced me that I had something worth sharing... and that helped me believe in myself.

To my lifers Pam Kahuda, Kara Mathis, Fran John, and Carolyn Capozzi—better friends I will never find. Thank you for accepting all of me. I am convinced that the countless hours of laughter we've shared have added years to my life.

And to Mike, Michael, and Natalie—I love you guys from the universe to the subway,[28] Thank you for being patient and picking up the slack around here while I was busy writing. I noticed, and I am so appreciative. When you write your book / screenplay / acceptance speech / inaugural address / whatever you want, I'll pitch in and do extra stuff for you, too. You are the reason I know that, in this life, I am beyond blessed.

Melissa, Mike, Michael, and Natalie Panara, July 2022.

---

28 How three-year-old Michael modified "I love you to the moon and back" to use the greatest distance his little brain could conjure.

ENDNOTES

The Blessings of a Bumpy Road

page 11   *Contrary to popular opinion:* Steven Bartlett [@StevenBartlett] (2020, January 23). Contrary to popular opinion, quitting is for winners. Knowing when to quit, change direction, leave a toxic situation, demand more ... [Tweet]. Twitter.

Takeaway Three: Finding Your People

page 57   *Did you know that the:* Mitura, K. (2022, August 19). 3 simple steps to help improve the quality of your friendships. Happiful Magazine. Retrieved April 16, 2023 from https://happiful.com/3-simple-steps-to-help-improve-the-quality-of-your-friendships

page 58   *If there is true belonging:* Miranda, L-M in Adam Grant (Host) (2021, June 29) (NO. S4 E14) In Work Life with Adam Grant. TED Audio Collective. https://podcasts.apple.com/mx/podcast/taken-for-granted-lin-manuel-miranda-daydreams-and/id1346314086?i=1000527201275

Takeaway Four: Choosing Your Perspective

page 75   *A negative or pessimistic person:* Merriam-Webster. (n.d.). Debbie Downer Definition & meaning. Merriam-Webster.

Retrieved April 16, 2023, from https://www.merriam-webster.com/dictionary/Debbie%20Downer

page 75   *According to the New York Times:* The New York Times. (2022, May 16). A partial list of mass shootings in the United States in 2022. The New York Times. Retrieved April 16, 2023, From https://www.nytimes.com/article/mass-shootings-2022.html

page 79   *Hawksbill Sea turtles were:* World Wildlife Fund. (n.d.). Hawksbill turtle. WWF. Retrieved April 16, 2023, from https://www.worldwildlife.org/species/hawksbill-turtle

Conclusion

page 95   *The false assumption that:* Wisner, W. (2022 September 14). Arrival fallacy: Will reaching a goal make you happy? Verywell Mind. Retrieved April 16, 2023, from https://www.verywellmind.com/what-is-arrival-fallacy-6561079

APPENDIX

page 101   *I am humbled to include:* Riverside Memorial Chapel. (n.d.). Alice Tenenbaum Obituary - New York, NY. Dignity Memorial. Retrieved April 17, 2023, from https://www.dignitymemorial.com/obituaries/new-york-ny/alice-tenenbaum-8043730

www.ingramcontent.com/pod-product-compliance
Lightning Source LLC
Chambersburg PA
CBHW022102020426
42335CB00012B/788